The Courageous Pursuit of Authenticity

Lisa C. Alexander | Nyoka Samuels-Gilchrist | Christine White | Dr. Carrie Young-McWilliams | Sabrina Robinson | Jackie Campbell | Shatriece Terry | Xenia Barnes

Copyright © 2024 by The Author's Journey
All rights reserved.

No part of this publication may be reproduced, distributed, or transmitted in any form or by any means, including photocopying, recording, or other electronic or mechanical methods, without the prior written permission of the publisher, except as permitted by U.S. copyright law. For permission requests, contact elona@theauthorsjourney.co.
For privacy reasons, some names, locations, and dates may have been changed.

Book Cover by michaelstar

1st edition 2024

Contents

PERSONAL NARRATIVES -- 1

    Chapter 1 | Lisa C. Alexander --- 2

Lisa admits herself to a psychiatric ward, risking vulnerability and loss, to start her journey towards self-worth.

    Chapter 2 | Nyoka Samuels-Gilchrist ---22

After immigrating from Jamaica to the USA, Nyoka fights to hold on to her cultural identity, sense of self, and authentic expression.

    Chapter 3 | Christine White---45

Christine's husband disappears without a trace, forcing her to rebuild a future for herself and their children.

    Chapter 4 by Sabrina Robinson---62

Sabrina confronts the impact of intergenerational trauma on her ability to foster healing with her family.

PROFESSIONAL NARRATIVES --**81**

    Chapter 5 | Dr. Carrie Young-McWilliams--------------------------------83

Carrie fights to prevent misunderstandings arising from her mental health condition from negatively impacting her personal and professional life.

    Chapter 6 | Jackie Campbell-- 104

Faced with workplace sabotage and politics, Jackie fights to maintain her reputation, risking potential conflicts and setbacks.

    Chapter 7 | Shatriece Terry-- 121

Shatriece challenges societal expectations and stereotypes by embracing her Compton background, despite pressures to conform.

    Chapter 8 | Xenia Barnes--- 138

Xenia's path to authenticity gives her the skills needed to deal with a toxic boss and overcome resistance to inspire change in the workplace.

Foreword

In a world that often pressures us to conform, it takes immense courage to embrace our authentic selves. Just as no two blades of grass are the same, each of us is born with a unique spirit. However, as life unfolds, societal expectations and conditioning can mold us into versions of ourselves that feel disconnected from our true purpose and potential.

As a money mindset coach for female entrepreneurs, I have witnessed firsthand the transformative power of reclaiming one's authenticity. When my clients embrace their true selves and discover their true calling, their businesses flourish. Aligned with their purpose, they recognize their worth and flourish beyond their wildest dreams.

Let me ask you this: When was the last time you were FREE TO BE YOU? When you are seeking authenticity and manifesting your dreams, it is crucial to know what YOU WANT, like what you REALLY, REALY WANT (in my Spice Girls voice).

This is where authenticity, mindset, and manifestation come into play. Your thoughts and beliefs shape your reality, so when you align your mindset with your authentic desires, you create a powerful force for manifesting what's best for *YOU* — not your kids, partner, or boss.

I have witnessed (I got the receipts!) how embracing authenticity attracts aligned clients, collaborations, and abundance. By cultivating a mindset rooted in authenticity, you vibrate at a frequency that draws in everything needed to support *your* dreams.

The Courageous Pursuit of Authenticity is an invitation to embark on this journey. Each author has shattered limiting beliefs, confronted their fears, and emerged unapologetically in their truth. I am confident that their lessons will resonate with you.

Also, each chapter ends with reflection questions designed to guide you on a journey of self-discovery and empowerment. These thought-provoking prompts will encourage you to dig deep, confront limiting beliefs, and give yourself permission to be free. By engaging with these questions, you'll gain clarity on your desires, strengths, and the steps you need to take to claim the life of your dreams.

Let this anthology be the inspiration to make a promise to yourself:

> Never sacrifice your authenticity for anyone or anything.

Remember, your authenticity is your greatest asset. So, find your favorite spot, settle in, and get ready to connect with the authentic power within you. Your journey to a life of purpose, abundance, and joy starts now.

XOXO Coach Jacqui

https://clearmoneyblocks.com/

Personal Narratives

Chapter 1 | Lisa C. Alexander

The Doormat Detox
Cleansing Myself of Toxic Relationships and Patterns

VOLUNTARY, SOLITARY SANCTUARY

After only a few minutes, my name was called, and once again, I made my way to the registration desk. This time, a nurse led me through security doors and into a private area. She stopped, asked me to remove all my clothes, laid paper pajamas on a steel chair, and left the room. I obeyed. And I cried. When the nurse returned, she collected my belongings and took me down an even longer hallway. She stopped at one of the doors and held her arm out, suggesting that this would be my room, and I should enter. Usually, that motion is inviting, and you anticipate stepping into a plush hotel room or checking out the amazing view from a cruise ship cabin. Not this time. I had voluntarily checked myself into Prince George's County (Maryland) Hospital's Psychiatric Center, and she had escorted me to my room, an austere space with colorless walls and no windows, electrical outlets, or decorations.

According to a 2020 study, approximately 2.2 million Americans received inpatient care,[8] — an overnight or longer stay in a

---

[8] Pedersen, Traci. 2022. "What to Expect From a Modern Day Psychiatric Hospital." Psych Central. April 12, 2022. https://psychcentral.com/blog/a-day-in-the-life-of-a-mental-hospital-patient#takeaway.

psychiatric hospital or psychiatric unit of a general hospital.[8] They seek help, hoping to find solace and recovery within the stark walls of these facilities. However, for many Black Americans, the decision to seek mental health care is fraught with apprehension and mistrust. The historical mistreatment of Black individuals in the healthcare system, coupled with ongoing racial disparities and a lack of culturally competent care, has led to a deep-seated wariness of mental health services. This mistrust is further compounded by the stigma surrounding mental illness within the Black community, making it even more challenging for individuals to seek the help they need. Nevertheless, there was no one in my life who could help me. In fact, it was because of everyone in my life that I risked a voluntary stay in a psych ward.

I was having a mental breakdown and needed to get away. But if you spoke to my friends and family, they would claim that it's been going on for years. In a sense, they would be correct. All my life, I've had this longing to be loved. I was raised by a drug-addicted mother; my siblings and I aren't close, and at the beginning of my life, my dad wasn't around at all. My adult reunion with him lasted only a few years before his death. So, I grew up around a mother and siblings who only cared about what I could do for them. From the moment I got a job at age 14, all they did was beg for money. They were all irresponsible, so if they managed to get a job, they

---

[8] "Types of Mental Health Treatment Settings and Levels of Care | North Texas Help." n.d. https://www.northtexashelp.com/mental-health-treatment-settings.html#:~:text=Hospital%20inpatient%20settings%20involve%20an,for%20less%20than%2030%20days.

spent their money frivolously. And when they found themselves in a bind, they expected me to solve it. And when I did, I wouldn't hear from them again until their next catastrophe. Neither ever offered to hang out or get our children together; after a few minutes of small talk, they'd get right to their sob story. Although I've felt used for years, as the eldest, I never refused them. They are my family, even though all eight of us had different fathers, and to this day, they have yet to return a single favor.

My family, though, was not the reason I checked myself into a psych ward; I was there because of my husband. Steven and I had been friends for twenty years; we had dated on and off for the first five years before settling into a platonic friendship. Throughout those years, he married, had children, and divorced. Twice. I was his shoulder to cry on, and his sympathetic ear was there through it all. So yes, I knew he had cheated on wife #1, and when he married wife #2, he cheated again. While still married to wife #2, he fathered his last child, the latest in a series of booty calls. Although wife #2 forgave him and desired to make the marriage work, he divorced her anyway. He always accused his exes of being crazy, but I dismissed him because most men call women that.

Ex Games

A few months after his second divorce, Steven and I were chatting on the phone and speculating as to why we're both still single when the conversation took a different turn. I had been spending all my free time and finances taking care of my mother due to her poor health, and I had recently moved in with her so I could provide additional care. And she was stressing me out. That's when he offered to take care of me in return. Given that he had already been there for me emotionally and financially, I knew what he was insinuating. Steven was flirting with me. I gave in just a bit; it wasn't easy. But I also told him that I was celibate and wouldn't have sex again until I was a wife. So we discussed the possibility of marriage and believed that the two of us could make it work.

A few months later, we dressed in Washington Redskins jerseys and made our way to the Virginia County Courthouse for our marriage. Feeling ecstatic, we left the courthouse and drove to Georgetown to celebrate our union with designer desserts from Georgetown Cupcakes. Neither our courtship nor our marriage was traditional, but our friendship was solid, and he had proven his loyalty and love for me time and time again. I truly believed he understood what it meant to be married and was willing to be there when I needed him. I believed I had married my savior and protector, a man who truly loved me. Isn't that what love really is?

What I didn't realize was that when I married Steven, I also married into ruinous family drama. His two ex-wives and baby mother were more than crazy. They were conniving, vengeful, and nefarious. They were infuriated when they learned we wed because I'd been a cause of dissension throughout their respective relationships. Each had accused us of having an affair because Steven would drop everything when I needed him. Their accusations never bothered me because, aside from a brief fling we had when he was married to wife #1, they simply weren't true. And even though I was well aware of his past and their current state of loathing for me, I trusted him when he was around his children's mothers and gave him space when he wanted to spend time with his kids. He was an excellent father to his six children, and he really wanted to be there for them.

To him, fatherhood wasn't only about providing financially; it also meant playing an active role in their lives. Steven made every attempt to attend practices, games, school performances, etc., and if they fell ill, he worked to be by their side. His wives were aware of his devotion and exploited it at every turn. The perpetual games they played as well as Steven's own behavior were not only driving a wedge between us; they were driving me crazy.

Ex-wife #1 lived out of state and called the house daily to harass me. She screeched repeatedly into the phone, saying that Steven never loved me and that he only married me for my money. She added that he wasn't going to be faithful because he still loved her, and our marriage would never work because I couldn't have any more children. Her accusations never bothered me because she was wrong on all fronts, especially with regard to my infertility. Steven desperately wanted us to have a child, but I refused. So, when she called, I gave it right back to her. I wasn't timid or afraid of her. But once I realized she'd never stop harassing me, I blocked her numbers so she could only contact Steven via his cell. But it didn't stop her. Instead, she got their children to call and cuss me out. She knew I wouldn't dare block their numbers, so every day when the phone rang, an overwhelming sense of dread washed over me, sending my mind and body into a frenzied state of fight or flight. Your home should be a peaceful retreat after a stressful day, not a daily battleground. But Steven refused to listen to how the harassment made me feel.

We were only married for three months when ex-wife #2 dropped off her three children to live with us. Two of the kids weren't even his! But Steven didn't care; he welcomed his former stepchildren into our home, so I did too. While we provided for them, she made every attempt to run my home. When I discovered their daughter had been skipping school and spending time with a boy, I punished her by taking away her phone. Ex-wife #2 showed up unannounced at my door and scorched me for disciplining her daughter. She screamed that I had no right to do so, then proceeded to cuss me out of my home in front of the children and Steven. As she slammed my door on her way out, I instinctively ran after her. By the look on my face, Steven knew I wanted to whoop that ass. But he restrained me and asked, "You aren't being godly. Is that what Jesus would do?" He didn't even bother to calm me down! I stormed off and spent the rest of the evening in the bedroom. I was in tears. He came into the room later and claimed he chastised her about her behavior, but I never received an apology, and her behavior certainly didn't change. He walked out without acknowledging my feelings of anger and frustration regarding the matter. He simply expected me to take it. Her kids lasted three months with us, while she received court-ordered child support the entire time.

The "booty call," as I like to refer to her, wasn't permitted to call our home unless her daughter was visiting. She could only communicate with Steven via text or email. This was all court-ordered! When their daughter visited, booty call ordered her not to eat my cooking, talk, or even look at me. She wasn't allowed to come near me, get in my car, or talk to her father if I was within earshot. Her pettiness wasn't acknowledged, though; I dismissed all that foolishness and helped their daughter with her homework, washed her clothes, bathed her, fed her, and did her hair. Once, booty call drove her own daughter to tears when she discovered we were snuggled up on the couch watching TV. After yelling and cursing the little girl out, she ordered her to go to her room, close the door, and stay away from me. She proceeded to call Steven and cuss him out over it, and she threatened to call the police and report that I was abusing their baby.

THE RECKONING

Everything I described was happening multiple times a day, simultaneously, and through it all, Steven had ceased being my lover, partner, and friend. And I became his doormat. If his exes or kids needed something, he dropped everything in our home and went to comfort them and meet their needs. Not once did he complain or refuse their requests. It left me feeling lonely and hurt. One evening, for example, Steven walked into the bedroom and looked me dead in the face. It was apparent I was crying. Tears and mucus were running down my face and nose, and I was still weeping. It was the anniversary of my father's passing; not once did he ask what was wrong or if I needed anything. Years ago, when he was my friend, he would have sat there and comforted me, even if I claimed nothing was wrong. Steven had turned a new, careless leaf, and it left me dumbfounded. I didn't know who he was anymore, and I resented him for all the pain and drama he, his ex-wives, baby mama, and children were causing.

When we first wed, I didn't work for 18 months, but when I returned to the workforce, I used my earnings to get him out of debt, ignoring my own debt. He hadn't filed taxes in years, and when the repayment letters came in, he refused to pay them, explaining he needed to give his children money first. So, I took care of it. The children he was referring to were now grown and attending college. He insisted on playing the role of "big daddy" and worked tirelessly to pay their tuition so they wouldn't have to rely on student loans.

With the amount of debt we were both facing, we did not have the income to take on such a responsibility. One evening, as I was sitting at the kitchen table paying his bills, I asked him why he stopped being there for me. I was surprised he even responded, but he explained that he felt guilty for not being a full-time dad. I told him it was a weak excuse for why he suddenly stopped being my friend. Then I asked, "Why did you stop being my friend? His response was silence.

Steven never responded to my question, leading me to surmise that he unconsciously replicated his upbringing. His mother became addicted to drugs after the death of his father, and according to family members, it was never the same. According to them, she appeared unemotional and detached. Steven never knew his biological father; he was an infant when his father passed. His stepfather had been in his life since he was six months old, and Steven always saw him as the financial provider. He couldn't recall his dad ever showing love or affection toward his mother. She was a full-time homemaker, so when his dad would arrive home, there was always a hot, fancy meal waiting for him. Instead, Steven and his siblings ate hot dogs and beans. They were pretty much ignored, and I think it hurt him that his parents cared so little for them; he strived to be a better father. But when it came to marriage, he didn't bother to do anything differently. He only wanted to provide financially, and he expected me to remain stoic while I took care of the house, the kids, and his emotional and physical needs.

Eventually, I did what every woman does when she wants to make their marriage work: I sought counseling. I didn't believe he'd agree, but I received no pushback from him at all. For more than a year, our counselor worked to improve our communication skills and provided objective input when it came to his exes and children. It seemed as if we were making progress. When we first married in 2011, I told Steven I wanted our bedroom painted purple, my favorite color. Steven never got around to doing it, although he worked to meet the littlest needs of his kids and exes. The counselor explained to him that the simple task of painting the room would make me happy. Having money in the bank wasn't enough. It looked as if a light bulb went off in his head. But soon, despair eclipsed my joy. The counselor then asked him to list the reasons why he loved me. He had no answer. And even more heartbreaking was that he didn't provide an answer until a year later. He confessed that I was the only woman who worked for and put in an effort towards the marriage. So, just like my mom and siblings, he didn't truly love me. He loved what I did for him and how I made him feel. I satisfied Steven's love language, but he had no interest in learning and supplying mine.

He visited me in the psych ward, providing further evidence. He looked uncomfortable as he sat in the visitor's station. Smiling sheepishly, I approached him and sat down to talk, hoping for comforting and encouraging words from him. Instead, his voice was irritated and impatient. Then he flat-out stated that I didn't belong "in here" and that he would have never considered me a weak woman.

I'd been the rock of the family for years, and he didn't know what he needed to do to fix things. After explaining that there would need to be outpatient counseling to help us through it, he shook his head as if he understood. After his visitation, he walked out without hugging me or holding my hand. I never saw or heard from him again.

Discharged with nowhere else to go, I moved in with my mother. A couple of siblings lived there too; actually, they never moved out. I got a job, and again, I was the only working person in the house. Each time I refused to give my mother money, or if I simply didn't have it, she threatened to kick me out. Desperate for a change of pace, scenery, and peace, I relocated to Dallas to be near my daughter and son-in-law. Tiffany was the result of my first marriage, and he had never loved me. We were young and dating casually when I got pregnant. His parents were religious and frequent churchgoers. They insisted we marry even though they knew we weren't in love and that their son slept around with other women. They didn't care. They just wanted to look good for the congregation. We divorced before our second wedding anniversary.

BRAND NEW ME

While in Dallas, I sought therapy for myself and realized that I had an anxious attachment style. According to a Washington Post article, there are four attachment styles, and the percentage of Americans who fall into them is: 50 percent of the population is secure, 20 percent is anxious, 25 percent is avoidant, and 5 percent is fearful. Attachment styles typically stem from early childhood experiences,[8] and mine formed due to my relationship with my mother. She was inconsistent in her affection and support, leaving me constantly craving love and validation while simultaneously fearing abandonment. This attachment style carried over into my adult relationships, causing me to cling to partners who were emotionally unavailable or mirrored the inconsistency I had experienced with my mother. It was a devastating realization to see that I was trapped in a cycle of trying to earn love from those who were incapable of giving it freely, and that my own self-worth was tied to their approval.

My therapist helped me move to a secure attachment style by showing me how to recognize my own worth and teaching me strategies to communicate my needs effectively, set healthy boundaries, and cultivate a stronger sense of self. Gradually, I learned to validate my own emotions and sought relationships that were based on mutual respect, trust, and emotional availability. So, no, I didn't just get off the emotional rollercoaster of seeking outward validation; I lit that b*tch up.

Armed with newfound confidence and self-assurance at work, I advocated for my skills, ultimately landing a director position despite my previous experience being limited to administrative roles. In my personal life, I found love and happiness with a man who truly

---

[8] Birch, Jenna. 2021. "Knowing Your 'Attachment Style' Could Make You a Smarter Dater." Washington Post, October 27, 2021.
https://www.washingtonpost.com/news/soloish/wp/2018/08/16/knowing-your-attachment-style-could-make-you-a-smarter-dater/.

cherishes me and shows his love through his actions every single day. We have established a relationship based on mutual respect, open communication, and unwavering support together. I also set firm boundaries with my family, refusing to let their demands financially or emotionally drain me. While the path has been challenging, I am proud of the woman I have become and the life I have created for myself. My story is a testament to the transformative power of therapy, self-reflection, and the courage to break free from negative patterns.

Lisa C. Alexander

Lisa C. Alexander is a resilient and empowered woman residing in Dallas, TX. After overcoming personal challenges and a difficult past, she has found happiness in her remarriage of several years.

Lisa finds joy in spending time with her grandchildren, daughter, and son-in-law and her two adorable dogs who bring her endless comfort and companionship.

Through her journey of self-discovery and growth, Lisa has emerged as a strong, compassionate woman who embraces life's blessings.

REFLECTION QUESTIONS

1. How can you practice honest self-expression in your relationships, even when it feels challenging or uncomfortable?

_____

_____

_____

_____

_____

_____

_____

_____

_____

_____

_____

_____

REFLECTION QUESTIONS

2. How can you recognize and break free from toxic relationship patterns that may be holding you back?

REFLECTION QUESTIONS

3. How can you cultivate a strong sense of self-love and self-worth to build healthier relationships?

Chapter 2 | Nyoka Samuels-Gilchrist

The Journey to Whole, Again

> *I am not my hair, I am not my skin, I am the soul that lives within.*
> —India Arie, *I am Not My Hair*

OUT THE GATE

As I looked down on the pavement of the walkway leading into the front yard of the two-story house, I thought to myself, "Could I make it?" I wasn't thinking about a cracked skull or breaking a bone. I wasn't thinking: Where would I live? What would I eat? Where would I get money from? All I was thinking was, "Could I get away?

Could I run away and never come back?" I stepped up into the window frame, then stepped down lightly on the awning just below the window. The awning's loud crunch frightened me, prompting me to shift my entire weight back into the window frame. I looked down.

I heard a shout in my subconscious: "It's now or never!" I chose now. I hit the pavement, stood up, and dashed through the small gate in front of the house that was close to the sidewalk. I ran... I ran down the main street, then turned into a side street. Before I jumped, I managed to stuff some underwear into my jacket pockets. I don't remember what else I spontaneously stashed in my pockets.

My adrenaline was pumping, rushing through my veins, so I didn't realize that it was brick outside. Brick was the term we used to describe the frigid temperatures that accompanied the winter season up north. I'm sure that "brick" was not a term exclusive to New York City teenagers of my time. The fact remained: I was a 14-year-old girl who wanted out of a world that my 14-year-old self knew felt like suffocation. This was my third run-away attempt.

Let me take a few steps back to help you understand the world I knew at fourteen. I am a transplant or immigrant — whatever term you use to refer to someone who was born in one place and moved to another. I was born in Jamaica and was essentially raised in a Jamaican household, as both my mother and bonus dad were born and raised in Jamaica. I arrived in NYC with my mother after she married my bonus dad, who, a few months before, filed all the necessary paperwork for us to gain legal residence in America. This was not unique to me. I went through every level of school with countless children, who, as I saw it, were living double lives. The apartment building doors, adorned with peepholes, single-cylinder locks, and Jimmy-proof deadbolts, conceal homes belonging to parents who were raised abroad.

In the post-war economy after World War II in 1941, immigration to the United States increased as almost 50,000 people from the Caribbean, both black and white, were looking for opportunities to create a new life crafted with the American dream.[8] Caribbean people came to work on Florida's sugar plantations and other farms across the US, eventually being infused into other sectors of the nation's economy.

Between 1941 and 1950, over 40,000 people came in from the Bahamas, Dominica, Jamaica, Barbados, Saint Vincent, and Saint Lucia, providing labor in 1,500 localities in 36 states. Across the US, there was an influx of people from the Caribbean, most notably Puerto Rico. The passage of the McCarran-Walter Act in 1952 closed the pipeline for immigration by black immigrants. The closure diverted 300,000 Caribbean immigrants to seek passage into Britain between 1948 and 1966. Immigration laws are an interesting topic because, as a country's economic status changes, so do its immigration laws. In September 1965, the Hart-Celler Act in the US welcomed the Caribbean once more, following Britain's closure of its borders. My family is a great reflection of the impact of immigration laws, as some of my uncles traveled to England when it was easier to migrate there, while others traveled to the US when the borders were friendlier.[8]

---

[8] The Schomberg Center for Research in Black Culture, Caribbean Immigration: New Waves, https://www.inmotionaame.org/migrations/topic.cfm@migration=10&topic=7.html#:~:text=Between%201971%20and%201980%2C%20the,the%20Caribbean%20as%20a%20whole. Accessed January 18th, 2024.

[8] The Schomberg Center for Research in Black Culture, Caribbean Immigration: New Waves, https://www.inmotionaame.org/migrations/topic.cfm@migration=10&topic=7.html#:~:text=Between%201971%20and%201980%2C%20the,the%20Caribbean%20as%20a%20whole. Accessed January 18th, 2024.

Having non-American parents offered colorful decoration to life here in the US. Parents who spoke Spanish patois, English patois, French patois, and African languages paved the way for vibrant ways of throwing down in the kitchen, child rearing, gender roles, and selecting career choices (which were usually doctor or lawyer). Parents didn't migrate to America for their children to screw around and be the second pick. These parents stressed that the plentiful opportunities in America were not offered in the small islands and other international countries where they escaped, so that they could "make a better life."

After I jumped out the window, my bonus dad drove out after me, expressing his disbelief over what I had done, and days later, I was on a one-way flight to Jamdung. That's the affectionate name given to the beautiful island of Jamaica in the West Indies. As I contemplated the jump, all I wanted to feel was freedom. I chose to sleep on park benches instead of a warm bed when I ran away because my freedom meant more to me than being so far removed from who I knew I was inside.

Before I left Jamaica at the age of 3, I attended a basic school, so I was as sharp as a well-maintained cutlass. Entering the NYC public school system in kindergarten, I knew everything required of a first grader. However, the only reasons I could think of for not advancing to the next grade were the thick patois on my tongue and the color of my skin. People teased me terribly because of my accent. People referred to me as an African booty scratcher, among a plethora of other derogatory and disparaging names that my subconscious struggles to recall. That subconscious place is where the majority of my trauma will reside for years to come. All of us undergo trauma and bury it in the recesses of our minds, where it remains hidden until it reemerges.

Migrating to a strange country and leaving everyone I called family behind was devastating. I have no memories of the first four years of my life. My first plane ride, buried under trauma. I lost the memories of my family as I stepped into a new dimension known as America. I lost memories of my family. This experience initiated the invisible cracks in my spirit that were palpable within me.

"There's no money in that" or "That's hard to get into" were the comments that would discourage me from what my parents thought were unacceptable pursuits in life. I settled on the sciences because they always intrigued me. But there were other twinkles in my eyes. I wrote songs and filled books with sketches of girls dressed in every style you can imagine. In my reflection, my writing and art were connected to remembering that life's potential possibilities were unlimited.

My mom would always take my sister and me to what she called "cultural events." On any given weekend, we would be out and about visiting Harlem, the Bronx, Downtown Manhattan, Brooklyn, Queens — wherever the culture was being held — we were there. Concerts, shopping centers, parades, protests, or lectures advertised on WLIB, the AM sister station to WBLS, which was on the FM band, guided our adventures. The Jacob Javits Convention Center hosted Black Expo in New York City during the 1990s. Everywhere I looked, I saw black people doing, saying, and wearing African things. African dances and drum rhythms awakened something in me that was asleep. The performers took the stage, and my soul caught fire. I wanted to jump up, go out there, and dance with the performers.

I believe that even though my mother exposed her children to the arts, she was not ready to see us fully embrace our artistic side. After all, "there was no money in that." They threw out my songs, leaving no room in my extracurricular activities for the arts.

As an adult, I often reflect on the difficulties my parents had while raising a family in America. My parents left their homeland, a familiar environment for a completely different culture, with no close-knit family connections to ease the load. The pressure must have felt like tons of bricks. Yet we are here, living now.

FREEDOM

The first half of my freshman year of high school unleashed a freedom I had never experienced in my life until then. I would tell my parents that I was going to school, but it would be somewhere entirely different. What I thought was freedom turned out to be where I learned how naïve I was about people and their intentions. This is where I learned that the way I perceived the world was not the way everyone else perceived it. My first real heartbreak happened during this time. I lost friends during this time. At this time, I was putting my entire life at risk.

My mother and bonus dad felt compelled to contact my biological father in Jamaica, gather my belongings, and relocate me to a place they knew would ensure my safety. Looking back at that time, I must say that my parents must have felt like there was no other option. I was unhinged — cutting school, failing classes, jumping out the window, running away time and time again — all within this short space of time, the first half of my freshman year.

Although my mother repeatedly stated that sending me to Jamaica was punishment, it was the place where my spirit began the healing process of fusing together my fragments. The warmth of my immediate and extended family soothed my soul. I was like cocoa butter on dry skin, quenching the desire for true community.

My grandmothers and my maternal grandfather were alive at this time, providing me with the opportunity to create connections with elders who I had no memories of after migrating to the States. I remember when I was 7, we got the call that my paternal grandfather had transitioned into spirit. I did not remember him because of the migration trauma; however, tears rolled down my face for him. When I was sent back to Jamaica, connecting with my grandparents filled a gap that my spirit needed to remember who I came from — where my roots were. That source of empowerment provided turbo-boosters for my healing journey.

What I found challenging was the transition from the American school system to the British school system in Jamaica. First, there was the commute. Not only did my sister and I have to travel from Linstead, St. Catherine, to Kingston every day to attend Holy Childhood High School, but during the season when the shortest way into Kingston was unavailable due to rain and floods, we had to do one of two things. We either braved the longer travel across the mountain or boarded with extended family in Kingston. Next, the challenging and exhausting road to academic success in Jamaica was another major adjustment. The grading scale was more stringent, so where I thought I was an A student in the US, I was a C student in Jamaica. Heading into 5th Form, which would be a sophomore in high school in the States, I selected the science track and began studying chemistry, food and nutrition, and mathematics — all things science because that is what I loved, and I wanted to become a medical doctor. After finishing that portion of my schooling in Jamaica, I decided medical school was not for me.

It's interesting to note that I wasn't the only child to receive a one-way ticket to Jamaica. Holy Childhood labeled a group of us as defiant and sent us to Jamaica for rehabilitation. Some of us came from Canada, some from the United States. After talking with some of the girls, I learned that some were escaping circumstances like criminal charges and abusive situations, while the rest of us were just so confused about where we fit into the world that we were depressed. All our guardians thought that Jamaica would fix things and fix us somehow, like a magic wand.

Living in Jamaica for a year and a half began the grounding of my spirit, which I could not understand then but fully understand now. That grounding abruptly ended, just like it abruptly began. One day, my mother called my father and told him it was time for me to come back to the States. No negotiation. I vaguely remember my father trying his best to talk with my mother about allowing me to complete high school in Jamaica. I was devastated. The family was devastated. My friends were heartbroken. I even lied and said my passport was lost so I wouldn't have to go back to America. That didn't work. I said my goodbyes to my family and dear friends I created a meaningful life with and traveled back to the Bronx, finishing up high school at DeWitt Clinton. My spirit shattered again into pieces in new places, different from where the healing had taken place.

UPSIDE DOWN

After experiencing a life of freedom, returning to a life that felt like captivity made my spirit a raging fire. I wanted my freedom again. The freedom that allowed me to frolic unmasked and raw. I could truly identify with Maya Angelo's book, *I Know Why the Cage Bird Sings*. My spirit was screaming to define itself, but everywhere I looked, I was being boxed in; I was being categorized. DeWitt Clinton High School accepted me as an honor student. Upon returning from Jamaica, I reviewed my transcripts with my high school counselor, which resulted in my placement in Macy's Honors classes. My Honors "friends" talked negatively, saying I thought I was "better than them." My "friends" could not see that I earned my place, and I was striving for a greater opportunity.

I participated in the college application process with another high school guidance counselor, who informed me that I didn't meet the requirements for the colleges to which other Macy Honors students were applying. My mother and bonus dad called a family meeting to inform me that, because of my behavior, they did not trust me to go away to college. The other reason was that they did not want to take financial responsibility for my potential failure. Do you hear the loud cracks in my spirit happening again?

My raging internal fire refused to accept that I could not do what I wanted to do, which was to leave NYC, attend college, and have new experiences in different places. I had been awarded a partial scholarship to attend Fisk University's pre-pharmacy program, but my parents ruled against my attendance. I knew thriving in a different place was possible. In my mind, I just left paradise and wanted to find it again, even if it was not in the same location. After graduating high school, I walked out of my parents' home with clothes on my back and moved in with my boyfriend and his mother in a small studio apartment at the time. If you know Caribbean culture, you know this is a HUGE disgrace.

What came after moving out of my parents' home was the beginning of opening myself spiritually in a way I had never encountered before. I connected with creating a sacred space — a space where I used the energy of water, light, earth, and air to connect with the divine energy nestled inside of every single human being, called by many different names but still the same. I know now that living in Jamaica heightened my senses and brought me to this threshold of divinity.

I knew intuitively I wasn't staying in the Bronx — I just couldn't see how. One day, while working at McDonald's, a stranger walked into the establishment and connected me with my biological father! That connection allowed me to travel to South Florida to reconnect with my father and make the decision to transfer from Bronx Community College to Florida Atlantic University in Boca Raton, Florida, to pursue pharmacy.

INSIDE OUT

Well, if I thought I had freedom in high school, college was wild! Yes, I had my dad close by. Yes, my mother's sister, my sweet auntie, kept a watchful eye on me, but I was 19 years old and charting my course in the world based on so many unfounded thoughts, feelings, and social constructs that were neither the truth nor a lie, just perspectives that did not belong to me. I was there somewhere, but buried under all of the noise of other people. College can swallow up young girls like me, and it almost swallowed me up as I accumulated more cracks in my spirit inflicted by heartbreaking relationships resulting from my naïve perspectives.

"More than 5.3 million students, or 28 percent of all students enrolled in U.S. colleges and universities in 2018, were from immigrant families."[8] In 2000, 1.4 million students were first-generation immigrants; those students were born in another country and migrated to the United States.[8] In 2021, 33.8% of foreign-born residents aged 25 and older had obtained a bachelor's or higher, with 13% of immigrants from Mexico, Central America, and the Caribbean.[8]

Years later, I worked with first-generation immigrant students who went off to college as intelligent, goal-driven human beings and came back diagnosed with mental illnesses — only a fraction of themselves. Their parents brought them to Wawa Aba Wellness Corporation for spiritual counsel because of the horrors they experienced while away at colleges and universities. Molested, raped, and violently abused, these young people were only a shell of themselves before college.

The Postsecondary National Policy Institute identifies the student immigrant population-specific considerations for success as the age

---

[8] Batalova, Jeanne & Feldblum, Miriam, Immigrant-Origin Students in U.S. Higher Education A Data Profile, October 2020. https://www.higheredimmigrationportal.org/wp-content/uploads/2021/02/Immigrant-Origin-Students-in-Higher-Education-October-2020.pdf, pg. 1 Accessed January 28, 2024.

[8] Batalova & Feldblum, Immigrant-Origin Students pg. 4.

[8] Postsecondary National Policy Institute, https://pnpi.org/wp-content/uploads/2023/04/ImmigrantStudents_FactSheet_Apr23-1.pdf, pg. 2 Accessed January 28, 2024.

of immigration, language, and legal documentation.[8] In my opinion, these considerations only scratch the surface. In my case, cultural, social, emotional, and mental health impacted my college experience. The whirlwind of navigating college life while learning who I truly was threw me into a tailspin. I had to be baker acted by my father, placed in a psychiatric unit and medicated. I was later diagnosed with psychotic disorder NOS. I always thought that this type of diagnosis must be popular among people who are admitted to psychiatric facilities with what laymen's terms call "a nervous breakdown." The diagnosis indicates that the presenting symptoms did not meet the criteria for a psychotic or schizophrenia diagnosis. Before this experience, I had not received a mental health diagnosis. What I know for sure is that migration trauma and culture shock are real, and when we dig deeper, these are considerations that impact success on college campuses across the country.

In my case, the psychiatrist that my family decided to work with had an interesting outlook on caring for patients. At that time, it was not a popular caring approach; however, Dr. Robert Vassall did a red pill, blue pill Matrix scene with my parents. He said, "We could go down the medication path with my treatment, or we could take a holistic approach." I'm sure my mother and father discussed it as I sat in the University Pavilion Outpatient Behavioral Health Services Facility in South Florida, a low-acuity facility, where I was admitted after being "stabilized" at Memorial Regional Hospital. My parents

---

[8] Postsecondary National Policy Institute, "FactSheet" pg. 3.

chose the holistic approach, and since that day, at 19 years old, the holistic approach to my mental health and my whole health has been a mainstay in my life.

After making that decision, I collaborated closely with Nana Mena Yaa Bradua, a traditional priest from the Akan/Guan heritage of Ghana, West Africa. Beautiful connections emerged from that choice my parents made for me, because I could not have imagined having to stay on medications that made me feel like a zombie, sedated, and numb, as opposed to the vibrant woman that I was becoming. **Queue *Vibrant Thang* by Q-Tip**

While living in South Florida, embracing more of my Jamaican heritage served as the lung tissue that gave me room to expand and express all of myself boldly and triumphantly. Learning and performing Jamaican folk songs and dances and visiting Jamaican landmarks like Accompong Town and Morrant Bay opened the door for me to dig deeper while studying Akan culture. The more I studied, the more vivid my dreams of past lives became, connecting the waters of this lifetime with previous ones. As I continue to learn about West African regalia, food, dance, and its connection with the African diaspora, I continue to learn about myself. I persist in nurturing these roots to propel my life forward, thereby enhancing the realization of my destiny.

The holistic choice my parents made was not an easy choice by any means. The medication pathway would have been the easy route in my case, but my spirit was not having it. My spirit fought.

My spirit was like a raging wildfire, burning everything down, ashes to the ground, so I could have fertile soil to grow in–fertile soil to create healing conversations with my family about how we would work together to place my shattered spirit back into the frame of my body; fertile soil to complete my studies as a graduate of Florida Atlantic University with a degree in Psychobiology; fertile soil to meet my husband and grow a family in love and understanding; fertile soil to return to school, get a nursing degree, pass my NCLEX exam, and stand at the same nurse's station where I was admitted as a patient diagnosed with psychosis NOS; fertile soil allowed me to care for over 20,000 people within my nursing practice and spiritual practice combined.

After I decided to return to school to study to be a nurse, my mother asked me about how my mental health history would affect my application to nursing school. The thought did not cross my mind, and the question did not present itself on my application. The question did, however, whisper to my subconscious a reminder that my mental health past should be kept a secret. And it has been a very private matter because of the mental health stigma until now.

On one of my many night shifts as a psych nurse, I returned to the unit I was locked inside as a patient so many years ago. I returned to moments from my past that I held so protected in my heart. I felt like I was in a movie. The nurses' station and the unit were empty, with no staff or patients in sight. The lights were dim, and the unit seemed more disorganized and cluttered than I remembered. The goosebumps and tears were inevitable as I stood on the unit. I escaped the claws of being 19 years old. This was the closure that I needed. This was the scene that allowed me to move beyond limiting beliefs.

The healing is never done when you live a life like mine. It is only constant balancing and recalibrating until new ways of thinking and being in my wholeness are formed. Sometimes I backslide, and I reach for the rituals that have maintained me for years. The meditations that my spirit recites, the baths with intentional herbs, the time for self-reflection, the dances that free me, the music that inspires me, and the travels that feed my soul with the knowledge of nature are all part of a beautiful reciprocation between myself and the larger community. They are all part of those rituals. When I forget, these are the habits that bring me right back to myself. Rituals that are unique to me and what my spirit needs. That means I have journeyed inward, and I know where my peace lies. I can access it whenever and wherever I please.

NYOKA SAMUELS-GILCHRIST

Mrs. Nyoka Samuels-Gilchrist, a Jamaican-born, New York City-raised nurse and mentor, exudes inspiration through her journey in healthcare and education. Armed with dual Bachelor of Science degrees in Psycho biology and Nursing, along with a Master of Science in Nursing, her academic prowess underscores her dedication to the field. Her career seamlessly blends compassion and education, spanning counseling for mental health to guiding nurses in onboarding and informatics across states like New York.

Having worked as a hospital and travel nurse, her diverse experiences enrich her mentorship. What sets Nyoka apart is her knack for simplifying medical complexities. She excels in bridging the gap between patients and healthcare by crafting relatable analogies and examples. Beyond clinical work, she's deeply involved in community development, contributing to cultural workshops, and serving on the board of the Wawa Aba Wellness Corporation. Her commitment extends to nonprofits like Women in Training (WIT), where her "WIT Guide to the Menstrual Cycle" empowers young individuals. Throughout her journey,

Nyoka remains dedicated to empowering individuals to manage their health. Embrace the opportunity to learn from her, and you'll discover not just a mentor, but a guiding light.

Visit 7healingwaters.com.

REFLECTION QUESTIONS

1. How can you create a support system that fosters your well-being and helps you navigate life's challenges?

REFLECTION QUESTIONS

2. How can embracing your cultural heritage and roots contribute to your personal healing and growth?

REFLECTION QUESTIONS

3. What steps can you take to honor your cultural identity and nurture your true self, even in the face of adversity or conflicting demands?

Chapter 3 | Christine White

Creating the Life I Deserve from the Power Within

It was December 23, 2015. All the kids were jumping on the bed and shaking me frantically. They couldn't find their dad. Groggy, I didn't understand their sense of urgency. No, their father wasn't lying next to me, but I figured he left the house to run errands or handle business. Todd was an entrepreneur, so he never let holidays impede a deal. He would get up and go whenever the client was ready to move forward. After more than 15 years together, I had grown accustomed to it. Our kids were teens and preteens at the time, and I was under the impression they had too.

Irritated, I got up and looked around the bedroom. There was no sign of him anywhere — absolutely no sign of him. His shoes weren't in the middle of the floor. His cologne, jewelry, and loose change were no longer on the dresser. I flew out of the bedroom and checked the hallways, bathroom, and living room for any sign of him. Nothing. In a nervous panic, I raced back to the master bedroom and checked his closet. Please, please, please. I flung open the doors. Nothing. He even took the hangers! I was absolutely stunned. He moved all of his shit while we were asleep. After shock and amazement wore off, fury set in. Not only did he take his things, he also took my and the kids' Christmas gifts! Things between us were combative, even from the beginning, but I never thought he'd pull something like this! Yes, this hurt me, but it just about devastated our children.

I said "just about" because the kids were sick of him. Since Todd's mom passed away, he'd become cold and demeaning, resorting to emotional and physical abuse for every little thing they did or didn't do. Once, he was so angry at the eldest child that he called her a b*tch because she cited scripture to prove that he was wrong. Before anyone could process what happened next, Todd was dragging her down the stairs by her leg! When they reached the landing, he looked as if he was going to hit her, but the kids and I hurried over and stepped in.

Another time, he punched the youngest child in the chest and called him a mistake for leaving his toys in the middle of the floor. He smacked our youngest daughter upside the head for leaving the front door open. The kids were unloading groceries. The kids weren't just walking on eggshells for fear of his yelling; they were accustomed to his verbal abuse. They had become bothered by the emotional abuse he inflicted and frightened about what he would do to them physically.

I was never emotionally abused or raised under the threat of physical violence, and it certainly wasn't something I wanted my kids to endure. My mother was a devoted, sweet woman, and my father loved her deeply. They raised me and my three sisters in a

Christian household and used very little physical punishment. At 19, we lost them both unexpectedly, and our home was never the same. My sisters and I were adults, but their loss put us in a depressive state, and instead of bringing us closer, we went to war over the littlest things. The constant arguing, mourning, crying, and stress were unbearable, and I desperately wanted to move. All our lives, we lived in an affluent California neighborhood, so it wasn't my intention to move into some ghetto apartment and struggle. That was all I could afford at the time, so I stayed.

Our parents left very generous wills which enabled us to pay off the house and go to college, but we all got jobs to split the household bills and saved what remained. There was no dissension when it came to managing money; we weren't going to be careless and lose our home. I am realizing now that my parents' loss and desire to live comfortably fueled my decision to be with Todd. And the fact that he was fine too. He was tall, slender, and had the deepest blue eyes I'd ever looked into. Unlike most Californians, he wasn't tanned at all. I liked that. From the moment he approached my table and introduced himself, everything about him and about us seemed right. It felt like fate.

I was out having dinner with my girlfriends the night I met Todd. My sisters and I had another fight over something incredibly small, and I left to vent with my friends. When Todd came over, we invited him to sit with us, and he and I hit it off immediately. My friends slyly gave their approval, and after paying our tab, I gave Todd my number. To say our relationship moved quickly would be an understatement. After dating for only a few months, I moved in with him. Then I got pregnant. This was our first child, and as soon as we settled into a routine, I was pregnant again.

After the second child, I was ready to be married, but Todd continued to stall. I had never been in a relationship before, and wasn't what to do. I loved him and couldn't fathom being with another man. We had to get married. To make my point clear, one night while he was away on business, the kids and I moved out of the house. I took everything: clothes, furniture, drapes, dishes, cutlery, etc. Everything.

Todd later shared that when he opened the front door, he was dumbstruck. He left and booked a room at a hotel. He tried calling me for days, but because I wouldn't answer, he began pleading his case with my sisters. After hearing his side, they eventually begged me to return his call, and when I did, he confessed that he didn't want to go through the pain of losing his family again. Aside from his mother, we were all he had. Then he asked me to marry him. I returned home, and a few months later, we held a small ceremony in the backyard. Fifteen years later, my husband pulled the same sh*t on me and our five children.

When Christmas Day arrived, the kids had forgotten all about the abandonment and, honestly, didn't care about the toys because there was peace in our home. After opening the last-minute gifts I purchased, we spent the morning at church and the afternoon with friends. I couldn't bring myself to mention what we were going through, so I sat around the kitchen table with the other wives while the kids ran outside to enjoy California's winter weather. The men assumed that Todd was away on business, and I said nothing to the contrary. When we got home, I headed to the kitchen to prepare a traditional holiday meal. The shock was wearing off, and my soul wanted to crawl into bed and cry. One of my boys took a break from his bike, ran into the kitchen, and gave me a hug. Then he exclaimed, "I don't need a father. You can be my mom and my dad." Tears swelled, so I didn't reply right away. I just hugged him tightly and finally said, "I love you, and we'll be OK." When dinner was ready, my children and I sat around the table, enjoying our meal, laughing, and joking around. No one mentioned Todd at all.

Months before he walked out on us, the children had been hinting to me that I should leave, but I never took them seriously. The house was indeed tense, and we weren't happy at all, but I never believed they wanted us to separate. My children had no other way of living. While Todd had always been stern and verbally abusive, he had reached a new low with the emotional and physical abuse. I figured it would stop once he came to terms with his mother's death, but it was approaching a year since her loss, and he was only getting worse. Todd and his mom were very close, and because I shared the same relationship with my mother, I empathized with his pain. Yet, I never condoned his behavior. I urged him to go to counseling, but he refused. Once, while Todd was home behaving like a tyrant, one of my daughters texted me a GIF of a woman pushing money from the palm of her hand, "making it rain." I was confused, so I texted back,

"What's this for?"

"You need to get your weight up and leave that man."

Notice how she didn't say her dad?

My daughter's text message brought up another problem. How could I afford to pay the mortgage and bills on a 5,000-square-foot home? I never finished college and was a stay-at-home mom until about five years ago. There was no way I could pay the bills on my administrative assistant salary. Shortly after the "making it rain" GIF, Todd returned my calls and promised to send money every week. But it was sent sporadically, so I couldn't rely on it.

Then his next solution was for me to use the credit cards, and he'd pay off the balance. This was a huge help, especially with the kids needing so much. Fortunately, the kids understood the gravity of our situation and helped the best they could. Without me ever asking, the teen girls picked up babysitting jobs, and everyone stepped up around the house. There were plenty of evenings I'd walk into a spotless home with dinner waiting. I was blessed to have such amazing children.

Spring arrived, and I realized I was happy that he was gone. While his emotional abuse of the children was new to them, it wasn't new to me. During our courtship, he spoiled me and treated me like a queen, but once we married, he turned vicious. He called me ugly almost every day and made fun of my dark skin. He joked that I needed to stay out of the sun, or if the lights were off, he'd ask me to smile so he could see me. He constantly reminded me that no one would want someone so dark, fat, and dumb, especially with five kids. He showed me pictures of his exes and bragged about how much prettier they were than I was. It shook me to my core, but instead of showing it, I learned to be just as cruel to him. However, the damage was already irreparable. My self-esteem was in the toilet. But with Todd out of the house, it slowly started to return. I noticed I was smiling and laughing more, wearing makeup and more flattering clothes. During a girls' night out, some of my friends even mentioned that I no longer walked with my head down.

When summer vacation started, the kids began asking to see their father, so we arranged for them to spend the summer with him and his new girlfriend. Todd had fallen in love and moved in with a woman months after leaving our home. His new love didn't change his old ways, though. Every time we spoke, he reminded me how stupid, weak, or fat I was. When we'd hang up, he'd send text messages threatening me to sue me, throw me in jail, and get full custody of the kids. He also warned that I'd get nothing from him, and he'd make sure that I went bankrupt and ended up on the street.

While I ignored his rants and never responded to his texts, I kept track of them all. I even downloaded a voice recording app on my phone, which transferred our conversations to the cloud. His words no longer hurt, and I intended to use them to my advantage. His threats about keeping the children didn't bother me either. Deep down, I knew he didn't want the responsibility. When the kids left, I picked up a part-time job and spent the free time I had recharging. The kids were wonderful, but they were also quite demanding. For years, I hadn't spent any time focusing on myself, and I desperately needed some self-care. I wasn't fat, but I was out of shape, so I joined a gym and made an appointment at a natural hair salon. I had finally decided to go natural. I also called my pastor and relayed everything that had been going on. He recommended that I start seeing a counselor, and I was actually looking forward to doing so.

The kids checked in regularly and reported that everything was fine. About a week later, however, I received the first troubling call from my eldest son. He was incoherent and crying uncontrollably. After calming him down, he explained that dad told him someone was going to break in and assault me. He wanted to come home. I talked to him for over an hour, reassuring him that nothing was going to happen to me.

Then, my eldest daughter told me she asked to go to church, and he refused. He began yelling and accusing me and my mother of being Christian whores, and he wasn't going to have her turn out like me. There were plenty more incidents, and that's when I decided it was time for them to come home. The kids had lasted less than a month with their dad.

You would think Todd was finished, but he was just getting started. Soon after the kids returned, I walked out of the house to discover that the SUV had been towed. The truck was in Todd's name, but he had agreed to let me keep it because of the children. Of course, I wasn't given notice; he wanted to make me angry and inconvenience me. I had to take off work that day, and a friend drove me to a dealership. I bought my own truck.

A week later, local cops were at my door, warning me that I could be arrested tonight. Terrified, I listened as one cop explained that my husband was charging me with identity theft. He asserted that despite our legal separation, I lacked the right to use his credit cards. I informed the officer that I never received separation papers and showed them the text message where he authorized my use. Both officers immediately understood the situation and advised me to hire a lawyer and continue documenting everything. They left without pursuing charges.

What was absolutely unbelievable throughout all of this was that Todd had been telling the children that he'd take me back if I asked him to come home. The kids loved their father, but they were adamantly opposed to our reconciliation. I was too, so I started divorce proceedings. Todd contested nothing, and the alimony and child support award were more than enough to help make ends meet. So, I did something for me. I pursued my PhD. For over fifteen years, I subjected myself and the kids to abuse so I could live comfortably. Today, I built that lifestyle on my own.

CHRISTINE WHITE

Christine White is a divorced mother of four who has demonstrated unwavering strength and resilience in the face of life's challenges. Despite the demands of single parenthood, Christine has remained active in her community, dedicating her time and energy to various church ministries and women's groups.

Recognizing the importance of personal growth and education, she returned to college, earning a PhD. Today, Christine serves as the superintendent for a mid-size school district, where she applies her knowledge, leadership skills, and compassion to positively impact the lives of students and educators alike.

REFLECTION QUESTIONS

1. In what ways can focusing on personal growth and education empower you to create a better future for yourself?

REFLECTION QUESTIONS

2. How can you find the strength to leave an abusive relationship and rebuild your life?

REFLECTION QUESTIONS

3. How can you create a loving and supportive environment for your children, despite the challenges of single parenthood?

Chapter 4 | Sabrina Robinson

Embers of Legacy
Passing the Torch, Shattering Chains of Generational Cycles

ACKNOWLEDGING THE LEGACY

What is a generational cycle? How can you break free from the invisible chains of generational cycles that develop into generational curses that are toxic to your growth in relationships, parenting, career, and identity? The threads of intergenerational trauma are intricately woven and passed down through generations like an ancestral heirloom.

Before diving into answering these questions for yourself, you must first find acceptance that much of your behavior, self-sabotage, and self-doubt are built into your behavior, your mindset, and your DNA. For many individuals, particularly those from marginalized communities, breaking free from these generational cycles becomes a profound quest for healing and empowerment.

In this compelling journey of my own self-discovery, during a season of mine that includes guilt, shame, and lack of confidence, the pages of this chapter unfold the secrets to dismantling the barriers that bind us, not only in your professional endeavors but also in the intricate connections within our relationships with parents, children, and girlfriends. Consider this a guide based on personal experience that will help light, ignite, and pass the torch to those looking to answer these same questions. Be prepared to expose both challenges and triumphs on your path to revelation and freedom.

Have you considered how long it takes to break a habit, let alone generations of behaviors ingrained in you by your environment, society, and family? The journey towards breaking generational cycles begins with acknowledging the existence of a legacy — a tapestry that carries both the beauty and wounds of the past.

Black and Brown women, often burdened with the weight of historical injustices, find themselves at the intersection of multiple identities. This recognition becomes the catalyst for change, an essential step towards breaking free from the chains of intergenerational trauma.

To break generational cycles, it is crucial to first understand the roots of intergenerational trauma. The historical injustices, systemic oppression, and societal wounds inflicted upon Black and Brown communities have left an indelible mark on the collective psyche.

> *History, despite its wrenching pain, cannot be unlived, but if faced with courage, need not be lived again.*
> — Maya Angelou

The journey begins with acknowledging the pain, tracing its origins, and understanding its impact on the present. The toxic behaviors and habits stop with you. You are what the bloodline has been waiting for. Here is the permission you need to start healing.

SURVIVING THE LEGACY AND BREAKING THE SILENCE

Survival is the first step in breaking generational cycles. It involves deep introspection, a confrontation with the past, and a commitment to resilience. Drawing inspiration from Audre Lorde's wisdom, "Caring for myself is not self-indulgence; it is self-preservation, and that is an act of political warfare." Individuals navigating this journey must prioritize their well-being. Prepare to grieve your past self and your family's actions. Prepare to let go of the built-in resentment that you have developed. Prepare to do the work. The work is painful. The work is exhausting. The work is needed.

Generational Curses are blessings in disguise: the mistakes were already made for you; now all you have to do is apply the solutions.
—Issac Mashman

To put my story of survival into context, I must reflect on a time when I was the primary caregiver for my parents for 5 ½ years. After I noticed a significant decline in their health, I moved them into my home. In 2009, they retired and moved to Florida from the Bronx, NY, to be near me and my family. After a few years of them living on their own, my husband and I agreed the best thing to do was to have them move in with us. Our three children were excited to have mami and papi stay with us. They were my kids' biggest fans. And of course, my kids gave my parents life.

We were three generations in a household, trying our best to function as one family unit. The true definition of the sandwich generation is personified. Slowly, we noticed it was more than just their physical health that was a burden, so we paid attention to the small "isms" that resurfaced, specifically from my mom. Silent treatment, emotional rage, explosions of emotions, and manipulation through money or gifts were all behaviors exhibited in the past.

The way my dad coddled my mom when she went into one of her episodes brought back a rush of emotions. When I began to exhibit these same behaviors with my children, something in me felt shame. There was a burning desire to stop this behavior, but I didn't know how. And at the time, I didn't understand what I was trying to stop. My actions were normal to me. It is what I grew up with. I soon realized that I had been living in a state of survival that was not serving me well.

This was the learned behavior I witnessed as a young girl that I blocked out when I escaped the environment — but it had shaped me. People can respond to a threat in one of four ways. Fight, flight, freeze, or fawn. I learned to be in a constant state of fight. But I thought my reaction was muted because I "grew out of it," but it was just dormant and came alive again when my past trauma found me.

That trauma's name was Mom. And so, history was repeating itself. The repetition of history reminded me that survival is an act of resistance against the forces that aim to prolong cycles of pain and suffering. I wanted to turn this response into recovery.

In April 2021, my parents passed away two weeks apart from each other. Unable to accept they were gone, I hustled hard at work, my identity shifting to the next label, my title at work. While 2021 was tragic, 2023 was a pivotal time in my life. That's when I held my highest title as Chief Operating Officer and was on the path to Chief Executive Officer for a mid-sized hospital in rural South Carolina.

I was in a very underserved community and always wanted to ensure I was an advocate for it. I represented hope for many in the community as a woman of color in healthcare administration. But I separated from that job in May 2023. I convinced myself that immersing myself in work was a tribute to my parents. But deep down, I felt guilty for taking the job to begin with. I had left my parents in my home with caregivers, and all I thought about was that my selfish ambitions were the reason they transitioned. While I was at work, I felt guilty for leaving my husband and children, two of whom were in the prime of their high school and college education, with my parents.

But without work, what was my new identity? It was the first time that I had to sit with my past trauma, acknowledging that it had resurfaced when my parents moved in. I was very good at avoidance and compartmentalization, so I wouldn't have to do the work. But I saw my children suffering from the trauma I was putting them through, and I was ready to leave the past in the past. However, without a distinct identity, my only remaining companions were my thoughts. I found myself grappling with a multitude of emotions. I was left picking up the pieces for my children, who are now having to face their own generational trauma. I had to listen to the thoughts that I had minimized while on my path to status. I dove into how defining my identity is imperative rather than letting my experiences define it for me.

I had always known that my mom's upbringing was challenging, to say the least. I heard stories of how she came to the Bronx from Puerto Rico as a young Brown girl, several shades darker than her mother, my abuela. There were stories of my great-uncles in Puerto Rico yelling at my mom to get off their property because she would dirty it. I heard stories of my mom bathing in bleach in an attempt to lighten her skin to avoid the abuse she faced from her stepdad, who was a lighter-skinned Hispanic. I heard stories of my mom giving my abuela trouble in her teenage years, and my mom's response was to run away, so she was put in a detention center for girls. I didn't understand the significance of the "why." Why did my mom feel the need to run away? Is that what I have been doing all my life? I dissected some of the symptoms that are common with generational trauma, including low self-esteem, hopelessness, a dependence on alcohol, and hypervigilance. It wasn't until years after my mom passed that I could understand her plight. It wasn't until years later that I appreciated the apology she finally gave me on her hospice bed days before she transitioned.

Survival is the first step in breaking generational cycles. It involves deep introspection, a confrontation with the past, and a commitment to resilience. To break generational cycles, one must break the silence that often shrouds intergenerational trauma. bell hooks, a prominent voice in feminist theory, reminds us, "To return to love is to return to one another." Opening communication channels within families, sharing stories, and fostering empathy are essential steps. Breaking the silence is an act of courage that paves the way for healing and transformation.

HEALING THE WOUNDS

At the intersection of accepting and overcoming generational curses, there is conflict. Planning your work and working your plan to avoid self-doubting questions such as "Am I worth it?" and "Do I deserve to be in this space?" is work that needs to be done before you can even attempt to overcome generational curses, as you need to understand where they originated from. What was the barrier's foundation? I empathize with my mom's experience of not having the support and protection of her own mother. Her childhood trauma came alive in her adulthood as she became a mom. I desperately wanted to prevent history from repeating itself.

I began to dig into the inner workings of self-love and self-appreciation and extend myself grace for the missteps that had already occurred in my life to begin the start of my new story. When I separated from my job, I went through stages of grief. I thought I was working through imposter syndrome, saying to myself that I didn't belong in that space, and it was too good to be true anyway. What I realized was that I was grieving the old me. The old me has been fighting the generational curses of past generations and trauma.

THE ROLE OF MOTHERHOOD IN HEALING

For many women, the journey of breaking generational curses intertwines with the sacred role of motherhood. Through the prism of motherhood, women find the strength to rewrite their narratives, passing on resilience, love, and wisdom to the next generation. This section explores the transformative power of motherhood in the context of breaking generational cycles, emphasizing the importance of nurturing a sense of identity and belonging. As survivors of intergenerational trauma embark on the path of healing, the responsibility of raising the next generation becomes a sacred mission.

> *Your life is already artful, waiting, just waiting, for you to make it art.*
> —Toni Morrison

Parents, guardians, and community leaders must strive to create an environment that nurtures resilience, self-love, and cultural pride.

Breaking generational cycles is not only about personal healing but also about shaping a brighter future for generations to come. My daughter is 22, and I have seen firsthand the internal battles that she goes through attempting to work through the pain that she doesn't know where or how it originated. Attempting to validate herself and reverse patterns that I played a role in her contributing to. I contributed to her current trauma through unmanaged, intergenerational suffering, including the pain of my own.

My two sons, 24 and 14, too, manifest feelings of guilt and resentment, passed down from one generation to the next. As I worked on my own healing, I engaged in a process of self-reflection, recognizing how my own trauma may have inadvertently burdened all three of my children in different ways. By acknowledging these emotions, mothers can initiate a dialogue that untangles the threads of guilt and resentment. Releasing the burden begins with an understanding that growth is a continuous journey, and forgiveness, both of oneself and others, is a powerful catalyst for healing.

Healing is a shared journey, and I intentionally wanted to strengthen my connection with my 22-year-old daughter, specifically by cultivating shared healing practices. We have and still undergo therapy, participate in meditation practices, and cultivate a bond that surpasses generations, fostering positive development in future generations.

Healing begins where the wound was made.
—Alice Walker

Mothers and daughters can embark on this healing journey together, as can mothers and sons, acknowledging the interwoven nature of their experiences and supporting each other in the process.

PASSING THE TORCH: RAISING THE NEXT GENERATION

The ultimate goal of this healing process is to pass down empowerment. I personally began to invest in myself, which empowered me. I forgave my mom, but more importantly, I forgave myself. I reclaimed my power and accepted the responsibility of carrying on the empowerment legacy. That light became paramount to my healing. The narratives of Black and Brown women illuminate the importance of mentorship, community building, and advocating for systemic change. Breaking generational cycles is not a solitary endeavor; it is a collective effort. Connecting with others facing similar circumstances involves fostering emotional intelligence and providing avenues for expression. Encouraging the exploration of feelings through a supportive environment where we can process our own experiences.

You have to act as if it were possible to radically transform the world. And you have to do it all the time.
—Angela Davis

Mentorship and community support play a crucial role in this transformation. Established individuals who have successfully broken generational cycles can guide and inspire those still navigating the journey. Creating a supportive community fosters a sense of belonging and empowerment. I leaned into my true purpose as I revealed my new identity. I started my own firm, which focused on career and personal development. I wanted to ensure I turned my trauma into transformation, not only for my own bloodline but also to assist those attempting to break their own cycles.

Passing the torch is not only for symbolism but also a call to action. My triumph is not just my own; it has the power to motivate and empower countless others. Of course, I am still a work in progress, as you will be. I am still unraveling the many layers of my past.

There are times, such as when grieving a loved one's loss, that I alternate through the various stages of grief as I uncover a new behavior that has surfaced. I now understand the triggers that can set off my past habits and behaviors. My family also recognizes these triggers within themselves. We have given each other permission to hold each other accountable. We apologize to each other when we overstep boundaries. We exhibit empathy when one of us regresses.

The power of saying "sorry" within a family is transformative, acting as a catalyst for breaking generational cycles and fostering healing within the familial fabric. Apologizing acknowledges the existence of past wrongs and, more importantly, demonstrates a commitment to change and growth. We have created an environment conducive to open communication and vulnerability. This emotional transparency paves the way for genuine connection, allowing all of us to address underlying issues that may have fueled generational cycles.

One final thought: for the Ortiz-Robinson family, we have overcome more than half the battle of acknowledging the legacy and breaking the silence. We are now faced with gratitude for our transformations and a sincere love for each other that will transcend through the bloodline. We are creating new habits and behaviors, new coping mechanisms for the trauma that is yet to be revealed. Our love for each other far outweighs our toxic past identities. We take pride in the responsibility of rewriting our family's history. We are left with the embers of the ignited flame to build our new family legacy of healing and, of course, love.

SABRINA ROBINSON

As a visionary leader in the healthcare business consulting sector and a passionate advocate for allyship and career coaching, Sabrina Robinson is a true example of women's empowerment and success. With a career spanning almost two decades, she has blazed a trail earning her reputation as a C-suite executive, strategist, and mentor par excellence.

In June of 2023, SNR Firm LLC, a business consulting, and career coaching firm was founded. Under her guidance, the firm's mission is to become a trusted partner for businesses, delivering innovative solutions that improve market share and financial performance. SNR Firm LLC's career and professional development arm provides intentional mentorship and allyship for individuals seeking to grow their career aspiring to enter the C-Suite. She also offers team development for C-Suite and Boards of Trustees members.

Sabrina is also an advocate for diversity, inclusion, and allyship. She has been a trailblazer in ensuring that women, particularly women leaders and early careerists, have opportunities for leadership and growth. Recognizing the importance of mentorship and guidance, Sabrina has also devoted herself to career coaching. She offers mentorship to professionals seeking to advance their careers and unlock their full potential. Her approach to coaching is not just about achieving career goals but also finding personal fulfillment.

Sabrina holds a B.S. in Accounting from the University of Phoenix and a Master of Business Administration from Florida Southern College. She is Fellow with the American College of Healthcare Executives and a Certified Medical Practice Executive with the American College of Medical Practice Executives. Sabrina is a loving wife and mom of 3 beautiful children.

Demetrius, Amaris and Darius, this chapter is dedicated to you. Thank you for accepting me as I am and loving me unconditionally.

Stay in touch at https://snrfirmllc.net/careercoaching-businessconsulting.

REFLECTION QUESTIONS

1. How do historical injustices and systemic oppression contribute to intergenerational trauma, especially for marginalized communities like Black and Brown women?

REFLECTION QUESTIONS

2. Explore the role of motherhood in healing generational cycles. How can mothers initiate dialogues that untangle feelings of guilt and resentment, fostering healing within the family?

REFLECTION QUESTIONS

3. In what ways do you see yourself passing down empowerment and creating a new family legacy of healing and love?

Professional Narratives

MISREAD MINDS

In shadows deep, with storms unseen, she stands alone, her spirit keen,

A Black woman, bold and bright, fights silent battles through the night.

Her genius, a flame that brightly burned, but for understanding, she yearned,

Her anxiety, a tempest wild, misunderstood, a troubled child.

Through whispered halls, her talents roamed, yet in her mind, dark thoughts loomed,

A mood disorder, cloaked in dread, a heavy crown upon her head.

But still, she rose; through pain, she soared, her every triumph, deeply scored,

In verses sweet, her story told a warrior's heart, undeniably bold.

— Dr. Carrie Young-McWilliams

Chapter 5 | Dr. Carrie Young-McWilliams

Misread Minds
A Battle with Anxiety and Mood Adjustment Disorder

INTRODUCTION

Mental health is a crucial component of overall well-being, yet it frequently goes unnoticed, particularly within marginalized communities. This chapter explores the journey of a Black woman grappling with racial trauma alongside adjustment disorder, depression, and anxiety, conditions that went undiagnosed for much of her life. In the circles of family and community where I grew up, mental health discussions were rare, often brushed aside with dismissive jokes labeling someone as "crazy" or "not all there." Amidst this backdrop, I found myself—a tall, statuesque Black Queen—deemed socially awkward by peers and adults. What sets me apart?

Raised in Mississippi, I was the solitary child of my father and the younger sibling in my mother's duo of children. I split my time between my grandparents, aunts, our neighborhood community, and church. My world was uncomplicated: school, my grandmother's house, church, and home. My social circle was close-knit, yet I frequently felt out of place, alienated not just by my physical stature but by a deeper sense of disconnection. I yearned for order and understanding in my environment, something easily achieved in the quiet company of my grandparents but disrupted in the presence of cousins or during prolonged interactions with church friends. Accusations of being spoiled or domineering were common, and the critique that I talked too much or over others was a source of pain. In response, I would try to adapt to others' personalities, seeking acceptance.

As adolescence gave way to young adulthood, my quest for acceptance found a precarious outlet in relationships with boys. This culminated in a four-year stint in a toxic, abusive relationship, where the cycles of verbal and physical abuse mirrored the fear of rejection that shadowed me. Breaking away from this damaging bond allowed me to find my footing and voice, enabling me to articulate my desires and thoughts without hesitation, a trait that the strong Black Southern women who raised me instilled in me. I learned to address issues directly, eschewing unnecessary detail in favor of straightforward communication. However, this blunt approach often alienated cousins and friends, limiting our interactions to brief encounters. When I spoke, it was with a directness that didn't always sit well with others. Those around me misunderstood my body's reaction to perceived threats or challenges, responses rooted in anxiety.

As a Young Professional

Embarking on my journey as an educator has been a path filled with both immense satisfaction and significant challenges. The joy of positively influencing the lives of young individuals has been the most rewarding aspect of my career. Seeing my work have an impact on their development, growth, and prospects has been incredibly fulfilling. However, I've faced hurdles alongside these rewards, particularly in my interactions and relationships with colleagues.

I received unexpected feedback when I took on my first role in educational administration. Colleagues expressed that my demeanor was intimidating, a perception that left me both surprised and confused. I have always believed in using my position to uplift and support, not to exert undue influence or cause discomfort. This feedback prompted a period of self-reflection, during which I came to understand that certain involuntary physical reactions of mine were being misinterpreted.

One such misunderstanding stemmed from the high pitch of my voice, which some interpreted as yelling or a sign of aggression. In actuality, anxiety triggered an involuntary response that constricts my airway and decreases oxygen flow. This physiological reaction, far from being a deliberate attempt to dominate, manifested my nervousness.

Another aspect of my misconstrued behavior was my tendency to speak rapidly or dominate conversations. This was not a reflection of rigidity or a lack of listening skills; rather, it was an anxiety-driven response. My discomfort with jargon and superfluous language often led me to seek clarity and efficiency in communication. I aimed to understand expectations clearly, convey my messages succinctly, and then move forward.

Despite these misunderstandings, I noticed a pattern in the feedback I received throughout my career. People repeatedly mentioned the same observations about my interpersonal interactions, highlighting a consistent misinterpretation of my anxiety-induced behaviors. This realization prompted me to reflect on how I could bridge the gap between my intentions and how others perceive my actions, striving for clearer, more effective communication and deeper understanding within my professional environment.

AM I BROKEN?

During a challenging period in my professional journey, people often mischaracterized me as intimidating, unapproachable, and even mean-spirited. Such descriptions couldn't be further from the truth, especially for those who know me well. My dedication has always been unwavering toward students and their families, particularly those who have faced systemic marginalization over generations. My approach, deeply rooted in compassion and understanding, aims to bridge gaps and foster positive relationships within the educational community.

I vividly recall a particularly telling incident that underscores the misunderstanding of my intentions. I had taken it upon myself to mediate between two families embroiled in a dispute stemming from a complex and strained relationship between their children at school. My motivation was purely to help find a peaceful resolution and ease the tension for all involved. Unfortunately, my efforts didn't translate as intended. A misunderstanding arose when one of the fathers, dissatisfied with the outcome, complained to the superintendent, falsely accusing me of raising my voice during our meeting. In reality, my response was a natural reaction to the palpable tension in the room, exacerbated by both families' frustrations towards each other and their perception that I had failed to protect their children adequately.

Despite my intentions and the nuanced reality of the situation, my side of the story seemed to fall on deaf ears. Rather than seeking a thorough understanding, my supervisor hastily directed me to 'make it right,' a phrase that resonated with a deep sense of injustice within me. The implication was clear: I was in the wrong despite my actions being motivated by a desire to help. This directive left me feeling disillusioned and disheartened. Now, I found myself under pressure to apologize for an action—or, more accurately, a misperception of an action—that I had not committed. This episode marked a profound moment of reflection for me as I grappled with the realities of misjudgment, the complexities of having anxiety, and navigating interpersonal dynamics within a professional setting.

EVALUATIONS AND FEEDBACK

Despite consistently receiving stellar feedback and evaluations in my role as an educator and administrator, a recurring theme emerged in the areas designated for improvement: I was advised to smile more, listen more attentively to others, and work on becoming more approachable and less intimidating. As a new school year dawned, it was yet another chance to transform my approach and address these feedback points head-on.

Eager to effect change, I initiated a series of one-on-one meetings with each staff member. I aimed to understand what mattered most to them and identify how I could support their needs as a leader. In addition to these personalized meetings, I established regular office hours, dedicating time to listening to any concerns or ideas my team wanted to share. I also committed to weekly catch-ups with my building representative to stay updated on any issues or feedback I might have missed.

For a period, this strategy seemed to bear fruit. I connected with my team deeper, addressing their needs and fostering a more inclusive and supportive environment. However, this intense focus on accommodating my teachers' needs began to exact a high price. I worked weekends and stayed in my office until midnight to keep up with my job's operational demands. This unsustainable pace began to erode my physical and mental well-being.

Depression soon set in, manifesting as sleepless nights, difficulty waking up in the morning, and a pervasive impact on my mood. My efforts to become more approachable and create a positive workplace culture, while initially successful, started to unravel as my health declined. This cycle highlighted a critical lesson about the importance of finding a balance between meeting the needs of others and taking care of my health and well-being. The pursuit of change, while noble, required a sustainable approach that did not compromise my health in the process.

THE WAKE-UP CALL

During a routine visit for my annual checkup, my doctor's unusually alarmed demeanor immediately caught my attention, setting a tone of unease. Wrapped in the less-than-comforting embrace of a hospital gown, I sat perched on the edge of the cold, steel examination table, a sense of vulnerability washing over me. Then, I overheard snippets of Dr. H's conversation, presumably with the hospital admissions department. When he re-entered the room, his next request took me by surprise. He inquired if someone could pick me up from his office, a question that seemed entirely out of context given the nature of my visit. Confident in my ability to drive and feeling relatively fine, I informed him of my capacity to leave independently. His reply, however, left no room for negotiation. "No, you are not fine, and I cannot allow you to leave in your current state," he stated firmly.

With a mix of confusion and compliance, I provided him with a contact number for a friend. Once Dr. H confirmed their imminent arrival to escort me, he disclosed the concerning reason behind his urgent actions. I was admitted to the hospital due to a combination of severe dehydration, an elevated white blood cell count, high blood pressure, and signs of systemic failure brought on by exhaustion. It was a stark revelation; my attempts to ignore and suppress symptoms of anxiety and depression had led my body into a state of self-destruction so advanced that I hadn't even realized the extent to which my health had deteriorated.

My friend, upon receiving the news, promptly notified my husband before taking me to the hospital. There, I was quickly checked in and placed in a room, one notably not equipped with a television to help prevent my blood pressure from escalating to dangerously high levels. The directive was simple yet imperative: rest, eat, and hydrate. Immediate intravenous fluids were administered to combat my severe dehydration.

In the days that followed, as visits from my children and husband filled the sterile silence of my hospital room with warmth and concern, a profound realization dawned on me. The sacrifices I had been making were not worth the cost. Separated from my family and the normalcy of life, while the school year marched on without me, I was confronted with the stark reality of my choices. It was a pivotal moment of clarity. I needed to prioritize my health and well-being to dismantle the unsustainable facade I had maintained for too long. An exit strategy was essential—a plan to safeguard my recovery upon returning home. This experience was a harsh but necessary wake-up call, underscoring the importance of choosing oneself and the imperative of self-care above all else.

I left that position that summer and entered into a few others where the same stressors continued to heighten my anxiety, which would raise my blood pressure and impact my mood.

This cycle continued over the next three to four years.

MY DREAM JOB TURNS INTO A NIGHTMARE

To break the vicious cycle of stress and anxiety that had come to dominate my professional life, I realized the need for a significant change in my work environment. I sought a role that minimized direct interaction with others, leading me to secure a position as a consultant. This new role allowed me to maintain my connection with the educational community while shielding me from the daily stressors of administration. The nature of the feedback I received was transformative, focusing solely on the quality and impact of my work with teachers, schools, districts, and community organizations. For a time, it felt like I had found my dream job.

However, three years into this role, the landscape began to shift dramatically. The onset of COVID-19 brought new challenges, ranging from the isolation of working in a virtual setting to adapting to the digital demands of remote work. Surprisingly, this period was a boon for me; the limited interaction with clients did not exacerbate my anxiety. Then, a pivotal change occurred within the organization: a major leader, whom I viewed as the cornerstone of our operational integrity, retired. His departure marked the beginning of a notable shift in the organization's dynamics.

I found myself placed on teams that required frequent interaction with colleagues who indulged in small talk and idle chatter—elements of work life I preferred to avoid. My desire was simple: to complete my work efficiently and sign off. Yet, this preference led to a significant confrontation during a virtual meeting. Unable to face turning on my camera due to the intensity of my anxiety, I resorted to using Zoom's chat feature to contribute. However, the situation escalated into a verbal altercation with a colleague over her meeting management style, which had previously triggered my anxiety. Despite a temporary adjustment that suited my needs for one session, old habits resurfaced, culminating in a panic attack during a Zoom call attended by several colleagues and a leadership team representative.

Recognizing the severity of my situation, I sought guidance from both my therapist and primary care physician. My therapist recommended seeking accommodations or considering a departure from the organization. Motivated by this advice, I formally requested accommodations that would permit me to collaborate and share updates through alternative tools like Slack, Google Spaces, or Trello, aiming to mitigate my stress and anxiety.

To my dismay, my request resulted in my being placed on paid administrative leave. After weeks of uncertainty, I was informed that my request for accommodations had been denied, and I was faced with an ultimatum: return to work under a "modified" accommodation plan. This plan implied that the organization would dictate the terms and usage of my accommodations—a notion that struck me as absurd. It was inconceivable that the organization could arbitrarily limit accommodations essential to my ability to work effectively. The comparison to physical disabilities highlighted the absurdity of the situation: just as one wouldn't impose partial accommodations on someone with physical limitations, it seemed unjust to restrict my access to necessary accommodations simply because my challenges were less visible.

This experience underscored the ongoing struggle for recognition and support for mental health in the workplace, particularly in environments that have become increasingly toxic and dysfunctional. It raised critical questions about the equity and understanding of accommodations for all employees, irrespective of the nature of their challenges.

I Thought He was My Life Partner

My struggles with anxiety, depression, and mood swings have profoundly affected not just my professional life but my personal life as well. After thirty-one years of marriage to my college sweetheart, a relationship filled with deep affection and shared history, I made the heart-wrenching decision to leave. While he always holds a special place in my heart, living together became unsustainable. Despite our enduring friendship, he struggled to comprehend the depth and impact of my mental health issues. Initially, I attributed this disconnect to his military background, reasoning that the rigid conditioning experienced by sailors, marines, soldiers, and airmen played a role. I also pondered the lack of adequate reintegration programs for service members, contemplating exploring this issue in future writings.

I prefer to refer to him as my children's father, eschewing the term 'ex' due to its implications. His tendency to cling to possessions clashed with the necessity for regular purging in our shared living space—a modest 2000-square-foot home occupied by four people and a dog. This constant cycle of cleaning, discarding, and reorganizing, only to repeat the process within a month, became a source of immense stress. Additionally, as the mother of a neurodivergent daughter who unwittingly contributes to the disarray, I found myself overwhelmed. The chaos felt suffocating, as if the walls were closing on me.

Working from home only exacerbated these feelings, as the disorder in adjacent rooms served as a constant distraction, pulling me away from my professional responsibilities. The dual demands of work and constant tidying proved to be too much. Despite my pleas for assistance, it seemed he could not—or perhaps chose not to—grasp the severe toll his habits and our living situation were taking on my mental well-being. I realized that staying would not lead to improvement.

Our shared Southern heritage and the cultural reluctance within the Black community to acknowledge and seek help for mental health issues added another layer of complexity to our situation. However, inspired by Maya Angelou's wisdom, "When you know better, do better," I recognized the necessity of choosing my health and well-being. This acknowledgment propelled me to make a drastic change, leading me to leave the marriage, the house, and the state. It was a decision driven by the understanding that, to truly heal and move forward, I had to break free from an environment that no longer served my mental health needs. This journey towards self-preservation and healing underscores the importance of recognizing one's limits and the courage it takes to seek a healthier path.

HELLO CARRIE... YOU ARE ENOUGH

As I navigate the complexities of living with anxiety, depression, and mood adjustment disorder, I've adopted a stance of openness and honesty about my experiences. Far from concealing my condition or its manifestations, I embrace my unique perspectives and strategies as strengths. My journey has transformed me into an advocate for students who face similar challenges, guiding them through the intricacies of understanding their rights and the importance of heeding their bodies' signals to seek assistance. By collaborating closely with schools and families, I aim to create an environment where students feel empowered to advocate for their needs.

Part of my mission involves engaging with parents and sharing my narrative to reassure them that they are not at fault for their child's mental health struggles. Through these conversations, I strive to alleviate the burden of guilt that so often accompanies parenting a child with a mental illness. My path to self-acceptance and effective management of my condition was paved with trial and error—a solitary battle to discover what worked best for me. Though intensely personal, this journey is one I am eager to share. I hope that by sharing my experiences, I can pave the way for others to recognize and address their needs sooner, enabling them to pursue and achieve a higher quality of life.

My advocacy extends beyond individual interactions, aiming to foster a broader understanding and acceptance of mental health challenges. By demystifying the symptoms and realities of living with such conditions, I contribute to a culture that values mental wellness and supports those in need. It's a commitment to improving my own life and enriching the lives of others facing similar battles. In doing so, I aspire to build a more compassionate and inclusive society where mental health is prioritized and understood. Everyone feels seen, heard, and supported in their journey towards well-being.

DR. CARRIE YOUNG-MCWILLIAMS

Dr. Carrie Young-McWilliams: a dynamic force whose journey has spanned roles as a dedicated educator, a supportive Navy wife, and now, the visionary CEO of Young-McWilliams Consulting, LLC. With her passion for fostering growth and empowerment, she co-founded EmpowerED Solutions by Young & Horner, LLC. Driven by her deep commitment to educational excellence, she pursued and achieved a Doctorate in Educational Leadership. But Carrie's talents don't stop there; she's also a creative soul, expressing herself as a blogger, poet, and captivating keynote speaker. Her workshops and coaching sessions testify to her versatility, offering insights as a trainer, mentor, curriculum writer, and presenter.

What truly sets Carrie apart is her unwavering advocacy for social justice and her unique ability to connect with people across a spectrum, from young minds in their formative years to those in the later stages of life. Her approach? A perfect blend of humor and gravitas. She draws you in with laughter, and with her compelling messages, she leaves a lasting impact. Her work as a National Equity Project Fellow speaks volumes about her commitment to equity, and her peers have celebrated her as a trailblazer in digital literacy.

Carrie's multifaceted career is not just about achievements and accolades; it reflects her genuine passion for making a difference in the world. Dr. Young-McWilliams is a beacon of inspiration, guiding those around her toward a brighter, more equitable future through the spoken word, a written line, or a strategic initiative.

REFLECTION QUESTIONS

1. In what ways can prioritizing your mental and physical health contribute to your overall well-being and success?

REFLECTION QUESTIONS

2. What steps can you take to advocate for your needs and communication style in professional settings, while remaining true to yourself?

REFLECTION QUESTIONS

3. How can you use your experiences to inspire and support others who may be facing similar challenges?

Chapter 6 | Jackie Campbell

Horrible Bosses

I wouldn't necessarily call Lindsey a friend. Work friend, yes. She never visited my home, and we certainly didn't meet up for weekend events. Now, we did meet up after work happy hours, and I was her wing woman. We engaged in gossip prior to meetings and shared our workplace frustrations afterwards. Our colleagues called us friends, and everyone considered us besties. However, in the end, it didn't work out that way. While I had no problem spending time with her around work-related hours, there was something about her that rubbed me the wrong way.

She never did anything to me personally, but I heard the rumors. She was cutthroat and wanted to climb the corporate ladder. People maneuver office politics, kiss the boss' ass, and work through impossible deadlines to prove their worth. Lindsey did all that. But she was also not the one to mess with. She took over meetings, interjected whenever she wanted, and volunteered to lead every high-profile project. She didn't socialize much, so there were only a few of us with whom she relaxed and let her hair down. Fortunately, or unfortunately, I was one of them.

We work for one of America's top Fortune 100 companies. Until a few months ago, I was working with a different team, and the team leader and I were friends. Kelly was direct and spoke up in meetings, but she was the complete opposite of Lindsey; she was fair and direct, and you always knew where you stood. The higher-ups liked her, and it was rumored she was up for the division director position. Our current director is transferring to another city, so everyone was confident she'd get the job. I also did everything I could to make her look good. I stayed late, took on extra projects, and praised her every chance I got. But for some reason, the division director had decided to transfer me to this new team. He asserted that this new team required my skillset. I voiced my objections, and Kelly tried hard to keep me, but it was a done deal. From the day I moved my desk, Lindsey started cozying up to me. That's why my intuition was telling me something was up with her. She doesn't kiss up to anyone. I wasn't trying to get on her bad side, though, so I played right along.

According to rumors, Lindsey disliked Kelly, my previous boss, before I transferred to this team. All the sisters in the office assumed it was a race thing. But when Lindsey befriended me, we threw that theory out of the window. Kelly was one of three team leads, and she was the only black woman; there were no minority division directors in our office. Now, there are minorities who serve in higher positions, but they're at our corporate location in Florida. We were fighting for it here in Chicago.

My new team lead, Tom, was simply incompetent. I suspect that's the reason for my transfer. I guess I did such a great job making

Kelly look good that they assumed I'd do the same for him. However, I gained insight into the dynamics of the game. I'm working to keep my solid reputation, but I'm not wasting my breath or my time on him. I complimented him when they asked my opinion, but I did not go out of my way to make him look good. Hell, in order for me to do so, I'd have to lie. Tom had been with the company for over 20 years, and in the IT industry, things change daily. I don't want to blame it on age because I have older colleagues who've been able to keep up, but it seems like Tom just doesn't get it. Or maybe he doesn't want to get it. A couple of us suspect he's just biding his time for another corporate restructuring and buyout offer. And to be honest, I wouldn't blame him one bit. But in the meantime, our team hasn't met quarterly or annual goals, and the corporate-wide system upgrade is being delayed because he simply doesn't understand what to do. If one of us led so poorly, they'd... never mind...

Whether or not Tom was a member of the old-boy network didn't seem to matter. He made the entire department look bad, and our internal customers complained. Tom isn't the most direct guy, and for the life of me, I can't understand how he was promoted to manager; he has no leadership skills. If I were Lindsey, I'd take over meetings too. But during the meeting we had last week, Tom was incensed. He gave Lindsey a stern look when she interjected, and then I glanced over at her. I just knew she had the balls to run him over. But she didn't. Her face was stuck, and she looked pissed!

Tom really didn't understand what had to be done, but he knew who had to do it: me. We were in the midst of a full-fledged integration project, and I had successfully led a portion of it when I worked for Kelly. The way he was explaining what needed to be done was just wrong, but I wasn't going to correct him in front of everyone. I simply nodded my head and assured him I'd do it. Lindsey and a few others were rolling their eyes and sighing regarding Tom's ineptitude. They attempted to include me, but I kept my head down. I'm not saying anything negative about my boss to them. They seem friendly now, but they're just looking for ammunition.

After the meeting, I stopped by Kelly's office to explain my new situation. She expressed confidence in my ability to complete the task on time and suggested that if I performed exceptionally well, I should consider applying for the team lead position. She'd have my back, of course. I gave her a few examples of the stunts Lindsey pulled, but she dismissed me. She confided that people were on to her game and didn't trust her at all. She advised me to watch my back, especially what I say around her. I assured Kelly I was and wouldn't put anything past her.

I underestimated Lindsey.

When you undergo employee training, they always advise you to lock your computer before leaving your desk. Most people don't follow this advice, and to be honest, IT workers rarely do either. We can hack and track anything and reason that no one is stupid enough to sit down at someone else's desk and sabotage another.

With all of the security levels our division deploys, we know who did what and when.

I received the project a few weeks ago, and it was nearly complete. Tom was thrilled with my progress and eager to put it into action. I could tell he was thankful and relieved, but he still had one foot out of the door. Much of his stress was alleviated, so he spent more time talking during meetings, and whenever he smiled, congratulated me, or asked me to explain something to the team, Lindsey fumed. But she was still friendly, and we continued to hang out at happy hour. No, it wasn't because she always paid. She's way too selfish for that. She was pretty and flirtatious enough to get men to buy us rounds. I didn't want her to think I disliked her or was gunning for the team lead job. Everyone knew she wanted it, and I encouraged her to go for it whenever she brought it up.

Tom and I met every week after lunch, and on this particular day, I was walking in from having lunch with Kelly. Tom usually ate alone at his desk, and when I got to my desk, I signaled that I'd be there shortly. I locked up my purse (I wasn't that stupid), grabbed my laptop, and headed to his desk. We exchanged greetings, and I logged into the new system, which would include integration. But something wasn't right. Most of the work I'd done was gone! Tom even asked me what happened and, in a nervous panic, said, "I have no idea."

"Well, was it saved?"

"Of course. There's an auto-back feature too. Wait…" When I logged in, everything had vanished!

Tom was furious and wasn't in the mood for excuses and explanations. All the bragging he had done to his boss was about to be exposed as lies or ignorance. And I didn't blame him one bit. I left the office practically in tears. I wanted to run to the ladies' room and hide, but instead, I headed to Kelly's office.

I broke down in tears when I explained it to her. Kelly handed me a Kleenex and asked to see my laptop. I pushed it her way, all the while exclaiming, "I did the work. How could this have happened?" Kelly remained silent until she turned the laptop on so I could see what she had pulled up. Kelly used her manager's access to review the actions taken on my computer. The most recent changes, the deletions, had Lindsey's employee ID number next to them! In seconds, I went from distraught to furious! I wanted Kelly to come with me to HR and explain everything, but she said she couldn't. It wasn't her team. And she didn't have to mention the unspoken ruse: two black women friends have no validity accusing a white woman of anything. Even if her employee ID serves as proof.

I exited Kelly's desk and made my way to my own. Before I could even sit down, Tom asked to see me. I locked my computer and headed to his office. When I got there, I saw our HR manager was seated in the corner. Oh my GOD! Tom went into an explanation as to why he's writing me up, and HR explained that I had 30 days to prove myself. I made it clear that I thought the write-up was unfair, but I could definitely complete the project way before then. "I decided to give the project to Lindsey."

It felt like someone punched me in the gut, but I refrained from commenting and instead asked to go get my laptop. They agreed, and when I returned, I pulled up the information Kelly had accessed. The HR lady was stunned; she even turned red, and Tom assured me he'd have a talk with her. "Because this proves I did the work, can I please have the project back? I already know what to do and will have it done even faster." Tom stated that Lindsey was already working on it, and that wouldn't be possible. I signed the 30-day written warning, grabbed my laptop, and went back to my seat. Lindsey's cube wasn't too far from mine, but I noticed she didn't once look my way for the rest of the day. I'm thankful she didn't, because I'd probably cuss her out or worse.

The next day, I waited until after lunch to head over to HR. I wanted to know Lindsey's status and whether she'd be fired. According to our employee handbook, this is a fireable offense. She assured me she spoke to Lindsey, but Lindsey couldn't explain why her ID was on your computer. She surmised there was a glitch in the system. She clarified that since no one witnessed her at my desk, there would be no reprimands or terminations. The HR lady advised me to spend the next 30 days proving myself and stop worrying. I left her office feeling powerless and infuriated.

Lindsey successfully completed the project a few weeks later, and they finally scheduled the corporate-wide implementation. Tom really wasn't waiting for a buyout. He had put in for retirement months ago, and with this project a success, he informed the team he was retiring. Everyone perked up, and it was obvious the Hunger Games were about to begin. I didn't want any part of it. I spent my days with my head down, saying little. Lindsey tried to be friendly, but I couldn't fake it; I had no words for her. Additionally, I could tell the latest office gossip was about me and my failure. I just wanted to crawl into a hole and disappear. We really need to institute a remote working policy.

Lindsey accepted the position. I kid you not. It was still within my 30-day warning period, and when we discussed it, it was clear she wanted to fire me. She assigned me vague, directionless projects with little or no guidance or explanation. She criticized me in front of the team and other employees and tried to discount every positive thing I'd ever done. The days when I loved my job were long gone. I was actively searching, but given the current job market, I wasn't having much luck.

Then one day, Kelly IM'd me to come to her office. Lock your computer! Haha. I still wasn't ready to laugh about it, but Kelly didn't seem to mind teasing me about it. After I closed the door, she said, "This stays between me and you. DO NOT BREATHE A WORD OF THIS TO ANYONE."

"Ok. Dang. I got it What's up."

"I'm serious, Jac. I'm not supposed to mention this to anyone, especially non-management, and certainly not to a friend. It could mess us both up if it gets out."

"Alright. I won't breathe a word. Anyway, I never let anything we said slip, so..."

"I know, but I want to be clear on this. I know you hate Lindsey.

"GIRL! She---"

Putting her hand up to stop me. "I know. I get it. However, she may be down for the count. Kelly unlocks a desk drawer and pulls out a manila envelope. She pushes it towards me, and as I read through the paperwork, I read statements from colleagues claiming Lindsey had deleted their work, shredded important documents, etc. without their permission or prior knowledge. Transactions on their computers had Lindsey's employee ID all over them. As I sifted through it all, Kelly explained that some even had doctor's notes proving their absence but had work deleted from their system — with Lindsey's employee ID as the initiator!

"Jackie, there was no way I was going to let that girl fire you. You've proven yourself as an employee and as a friend. I know the corporate world is cutthroat, and dealing with people like Lindsey is common, but sometimes you have to go out on a limb and do what's right."

"Thank you, Kelly. Seriously. No one has stood up for me before. Everyone is all about themselves."

"Don't I know it? It's worse in management. What's really trifling is that Tom has been fielding complaints about Lindsey for years! When we traded you and Meghan, it was one of the first things she mentioned to me. Tom did absolutely nothing about her, allowing her to do whatever she wanted. That's why I kept telling you to watch your back. I also assumed you always locked your computer. Remember me stressing that after every meeting?"

"Yeah."

"Don't worry. I got you. Another manager and I spoke with HR, and they're doing a full investigation. Just keep doing great work, stay positive, and LOCK YOUR COMPUTER."

Currently, HR is investigating Lindsey.

JACKIE CAMPBELL

Meet Jackie Campbell, a dynamic IT professional with a zest for life both on and off the computer screen. Happily married, Jackie shares her home with her beloved husband and their adorable Yorkie. When Jackie isn't tackling complex tech challenges at work, you can find her pounding the pavement as an avid marathoner.

But Jackie's talents don't stop there. She's also a self-proclaimed vegan chef, whipping up delectable plant-based dishes. Her husband, however, remains skeptical, often joking that he'd rather eat his own running shoes than her "grass-fed" delights. Despite their dietary differences, Jackie and her husband's love for each other (and their Yorkie) keeps their household filled with laughter and happiness.

REFLECTION QUESTIONS

1. In what ways can you maintain your integrity and consistency in your professional life, even when faced with challenges or adversity?

REFLECTION QUESTIONS

2. In what ways can building strong, supportive relationships with colleagues help you overcome professional obstacles?

REFLECTION QUESTIONS

3. How can you use your experiences to advocate for positive change and fairness in the workplace?

Chapter 7 | Shatriece Terry

The Power of Identity
Compton to Corporate Mentor by Overcoming Self-Doubt

We build our temples for tomorrow, as strong as we know how, and we stand on top of the mountain, free within ourselves.
— Langston Hughes

IDENTITY

My journey from Compton to corporate was a struggle for identity and belonging. Crime, gangs, drugs, and poverty. It's mostly true. My childhood was challenging. My sister and I spent most of it moving from one couch to another and talking to judges about which of our alcoholic parents would get custody. How could someone like me become a corporate executive earning six figures? Well, it definitely wasn't easy.

Growing up in Compton during the 1980s, cultural and social forces had a significant impact on me. Before I got a passport, my first means of travel was rap music, which served as a guide in my search for belonging. In 1989, N.W.A.'s *Straight Outta Compton* video was an inspiration, with its burning images of the rebellion against police brutality as a statement of fact — I am not what you perceive me to be. Without a role model, those lyrics helped me identify who I was and wanted to become. On the surface, we often believe what others see or think about us for who we are. We absorb their opinions and assumptions, allowing ourselves to fit into a perceived identity.

Like most new college graduates from the University of Southern California, I jumped right into the workforce, powering through entry-level positions by outperforming my peers and toting productivity as the magic key to getting a promotion. Soon, I was a finalist for "Employee of the Year" and had a corner office with floor-to-ceiling glass windows on the top floor.

Being the only Black woman in the room made the journey harder to navigate because I didn't have anyone who understood or had "been there" to guide me. I was trying to thrive in predominantly white and male spaces without a mentor.

I remember funny and awkward moments trying to fit in. Like my first job interview over lunch, I was concerned about what I should order so I wouldn't look inexperienced. I had to figure out how to get a $255 cash advance loan the first time I traveled for work. During a stressful client dinner meeting, I frantically checked my credit card balance, unaware that the highest-ranking manager at the table held the privilege. I'm happy to report that I successfully navigated that situation, along with several others.

After these seemingly insurmountable setbacks, I emerged with a powerful lesson: Embracing your cultural heritage is a powerful source of strength and identity. My cultural background is a source of immense strength.

To achieve in corporate America, I leverage the same skills I honed in Compton: the resilience to bounce back from setbacks like a missed promotion, the street smarts to navigate complex office politics, and the situational awareness to read the room. Self-discovery often requires allowing ourselves to be vulnerable and shedding the masks we wear to please others.

My Best Advice Is:
Identify who you are and who you will become.

ALLOWING

I have high anxiety about allowing others to help me. They taught me that asking for help is a sign of weakness. Like impostor syndrome, I'm uncomfortable because I don't feel that others see me as special or worthy. I also mistakenly equated someone's assistance with their selection of me. I thought that being picked was an act that someone else could give to me. What actually happens is that I am allowing them to choose me. On my behalf, I am allowing them to remove roadblocks.

It's a difficult thing — the possibility of "allowing it." "It" is the thing I most deeply desire in this world. The thing that would make me feel whole, seen, loved, and chosen. I lost my childhood at a young age —the magic of freedom to believe and allow dreams into my consciousness and body. To feel something in my body makes it real. Feeling is similar to sound — a vibration that only I can quantify. Allowing is new for me because there was rarely a time in my life when I was free to allow the possibility of imagination. As an adult, I carried this with me, which shows up in how I move around in corporate.

I had to relearn and unlearn what it means to be chosen. When I feel like I am waiting, I remind myself of my true self and develop a new narrative:

My past self: I am in the room waiting to be chosen, compared to someone or something else that grabs their attention. They could be a parent, a partner, or a manager at work. It looks like waiting.

My true self: I am in the room, allowing them to choose me. I am the prize. To believe and allow is not a small thing. To believe is to allow myself to take up space in my body, mind, and soul, and call on my community to stand with me in this space. I ask. I am no longer waiting. I no longer think about what is good for them. I think about what is good for me.

My Best Advice Is:
Allow yourself to be chosen.

WORTHY

It was promotion season at my company in late February. They held my promotion to senior director at gunpoint. I sat in the office of the Chief Operating Officer, my boss, and the Vice President of Human Resources. *"Am I being fired?"* I asked point-blank. It was a legitimate question. I'm the highest-ranking Black person in the company after eight years of service, and I'm being called to the "principal's office." The company elevated every leader in my division from director to senior director. That is every leader except me, and I was the only one reporting directly to the c-suite. All of my peers had either AVP or VP titles. I sat there, looking out the glass window onto the most beautifully landscaped quad in Santa Monica, and waited for an answer. The HR President started first.

"No, you're not being fired," she said. "A fellow director has reported that he doesn't like you because of a decision you made." "Liking me is not a part of my job description," I replied. "My boss asked me to solve the problem, and I did. Furthermore, it is not that he doesn't like me. He doesn't know me. I am quite likeable. I have swag. He doesn't like me telling him how to do his job." "I agree with you," my boss interrupted. "We simply wanted to address this as an area for improvement before telling you that we're promoting you and giving you a raise." Congratulations."

The experience was both painful and clarifying. I walked out of the office that day, not surprised but frustrated. It wasn't the first time they held my promotion at gunpoint. Still, I was determined not to give up and leave the workplace.

Everyone dreams of a fulfilled life, even (or especially) those without a mentor.

In the introduction, I mentioned I grew up in Compton, California. Compton is a place, but Compton is also my identity. My state of mind. That same image most people have about "someone from Compton" was also how I saw myself. At the same time, I knew deep down that I was different. I was more than "Compton." I needed to get out of that identity box to have an abundant life. As I started to forge my own way, I developed my own identity to break free of other people's assumptions.

I was not an imposter; I was an outsider.

Women of color often fight many internal and external battles to get ahead. I spent a long time healing from the wounds of my past, building confidence in myself and my talents, and learning to believe I belong in any room I walk into. My journey led me to a six-figure position and motivated me to share my experiences with others so they could have the life and career they desired. I became a role model to guide women into excellence and advocate for pay equity for Black women in corporate America.

My Best Advice Is:
Know that you are worthy of a good and healthy career.

MENTORING

The politics of knowledge have imprisoned Black folks and women in the United States since 1740. Anti-literacy laws made it illegal for enslaved and free people of color to read or write, and Title IX was needed to transform women's education, leveling the playing field in sports and allowing millions of women to earn college degrees in 1972. Because of that revolutionary social change, the percentage of women between the ages of 25 and 34 with at least a college degree has more than tripled since 1968.[8]

"We know that mentorship is essential to the growth of young professionals. The evidence is clear: 75% of executives credit their success to advisors, and recent research shows that 90% of employees with a career guide are happy at work. Despite this, and despite the fact that 84% of U.S. Fortune 500 firms leverage programs, the majority of these programs fail employees from marginalized communities. Most women of color either fail to reach the management level or plateau in middle management."[8]

"The glass ceiling" is the name given to social barriers preventing women from top jobs in management, and "the broken rung" is a metaphor for the disparity in promotions for women of color from entry-level to manager (whereas being denied access to the first rung on the ladder is the broken rung).

I was mid-level in my career as Manager of Operations, and I was quickly moving up the ladder. New hires would email me or approach me in the hallway to inquire about my promotion. The growing number of colleagues became too much to manage individually, so I started the Black Employee Resource Group (ERG) to share knowledge in a group format. Each member of our

---

[8] Equal Access to Education: Forty Years of Title IX, United States Department of Justice 2012

[8] Christopher "CJ" Gross, A better approach to mentorship, Harvard Business Review, 2023

tight-knit peer support group contributed to each other's advancement by sharing the unwritten rules for promotion.

Marie Devaux, a black businesswoman, explains why there is a need for the best employee communities: I tend to gravitate toward marginalized communities. Because I feel like we have a lot in common in that space. We can understand each other's struggles, and we are also dealing with privilege in our work and in our businesses in a very different way.[8]

Looking at the dynamics in a hierarchical relationship, we know that the mentee could feel like she is in a vulnerable position. It feels like someone is doing them a favor or that she is a weak link needing assistance. This is not true. Being a mentor allows others to practice leadership by working to offer support and direction while helping them learn and evolve in the process.

My Best Advice Is:
Find your mentor, be a mentor, and boss up together.

ACTIVIST

In 2020, the Black Lives Matter™ movement shook the world, and the harsh reality of being paid $0.67 on the dollar catapulted me to get off the career ladder and into mission-driven work. The vision took form with the launch of Promote Black Women™.

---

[8] Marie DeVaux, Finding Your Tribe as a Black Business Woman, 2019

Galvanized by the racial justice protests sweeping the nation after George Floyd's murder, the social impact organization's mission is to accelerate advancement for Black career women through highly tailored mentoring programs. Mentoring is a kind of nurturing whereby they help or motivate the mentee to construct a vision of possibilities beyond the present moment."[8]

The Harvard Business Review agrees that "leveling the playing field with mentoring has the potential to empower marginalized communities, enhance talent retention, strengthen succession pipelines, and build cultures of belonging."[8] It creates a shortcut through the nonsense and crafts a true path to professional success with tailored conversations on equity, exposure, and communication. Role models are activists who organize change and become architects of their legacy. Our chants pave the way for change.

An activist raises awareness about community needs. As part of my activism, I became a leader in the Black Employee Resource Group (ERG). We engage in activism because we are sick and tired of something we love being stolen: the planet, clean air, human rights, and exploitation.

The genesis of activism is to have a better world for our children and youth, wanting to improve the world for future generations by

---

[8] Gail Y Okawa, Diving for Pearls: Mentoring as Cultural and Activist Practice among Academics of Color, 2002

[8] Christopher "CJ" Gross, A better approach to mentorship, Harvard Business Review, 2023

grooming younger generations to be better than we are now. Black women have a powerful legacy of activism, from advocating for themselves in the workplace to fighting for systemic change. By standing up for yourself, you not only create a better space for yourself but also inspire and empower others in your community.

My Best Advice Is:
Advocate for yourself with courage.

FINAL WORDS

When we embrace our authenticity and the unique challenges it presents, we strengthen not just our identity, but we also pave the way for others. This self-assurance becomes the foundation for powerful activism, and when channeled into mentorship, it ignites a ripple effect of empowerment that will transform our families, communities, and entire nations.

SHATRIECE TERRY

Shatriece Terry is a multifaceted force in women's empowerment and advocacy. As an author, mentor, and speaker, she has dedicated her life's work to uplifting women, particularly Black women, in their professional pursuits. Shatriece's guidance is instrumental in helping women master the corporate climb™, breaking through glass ceilings, and securing well-deserved promotions. At the helm of Promote Black Women™, Shatriece spearheads a groundbreaking initiative to dismantle the pervasive gender pay gap through a unique blend of social action and mentorship.

In a landscape where systemic barriers often hinder women's advancement, Shatriece Terry stands as a beacon of hope and resilience. Her visionary leadership with Promote Black Women™ not only addresses the pressing issue of pay disparity but also cultivates a community of support and empowerment. Join Shatriece in her mission to promote equality and support women's advancement in the workplace.

Originally from Compton, California, she has lived and worked in Miami and now calls Atlanta home.

Stay in touch at www.shatriece.com.

REFLECTION QUESTIONS

1. How has your background and life experiences shaped your identity? In what ways have you struggled to reconcile your authentic self with societal expectations, especially in professional settings?

_____

_____

_____

_____

_____

_____

_____

_____

_____

_____

_____

_____

_____

_____

REFLECTION QUESTIONS

2. How comfortable are you with vulnerability and seeking support? What steps can you take to "allow" yourself to be chosen and reach out for assistance when needed?

REFLECTION QUESTIONS

3. What would it look like to courageously embrace your authenticity in all aspects of your life, and how might this contribute to your personal and professional fulfillment?

Chapter 8 | Xenia Barnes

Authenticity as an Act of Revolution

She was heading my way, swirling the ends of her hair between her fingers as they so often do. My teeth clenched, and I mentally rolled my eyes, thinking, "Here comes the bullsh*t!"

I had just left the school leadership meeting, and I only had 5 minutes before teachers would enter the room before the weekly professional development session. For three years, I worked on the school culture team, reporting to her. Our relationship was rocky, to say the least.

As she got closer, I smirked and slid on my invisible mask as the words came slithering out of "Karen's" privileged mouth. "Ms. Barnes, I somehow get the feeling that you just are not being your authentic self in the meetings." Oh, she tried it!

'B*tch, please!' echoed in my head as I felt steam rising through my body. Then I thought, "Well, look at Captain Obvious! Why would I give her access to my authentic self when she still hasn't increased my salary to match the brilliance I bring to every talk, meeting, professional development workshop, parent conference—and let's not even get started on the infuriating refrain of 'Let's ask Ms. Barnes what Black parents need to discuss?' How racist! Did they really expect me to be the voice of every single Black parent whose children attended this school? Because that assumption set me off, I always held my breath and counted to 10 before responding, "How about we do a survey and ask parents for topics they'd be interested in, or maybe utilize the PTA to come up with ideas?"

So here she was with another racist comment. I counted to 10 to keep my cool and do my job, then swirled the ends of my hair between my fingers—just like she did—and smiled. "I guess we'll never know," and she walked away.

THE AUTHENTICITY TRAP

In the past, I could never determine whether "showing up as your authentic self" was performative and part of a hidden corporate agenda against people of color. As I navigated 10 years of leadership roles as an educator, dean, and supervisor with gaslighting supervisors and workplace mobbing, the phrase triggers me today. It's a setup, y'all!

While I would have liked to believe Karen's request for me to show up authentically was coming from a place of caring and support, there are too many statistics that show otherwise. Research has consistently shown that Black job applicants with natural, African-style hair face more negative assessments by hiring managers, being perceived as more aggressive and less professional, which suggests the impact of racial prejudices on views of employment.[8] Black professionals also

---

[8] "Research Suggests Bias Against Natural Hair Limits Job Opportunities for Black Women." n.d. Duke's Fuqua School of Business. https://www.fuqua.duke.edu/duke-fuqua-insights/ashleigh-rosette-research-suggests-bias-against-natural-hair-limits-job.

remain significantly more likely to be fired or laid off than their white colleagues in today's organizations.[8]

The consequences I immediately feared when she made that comment included losing my job, stalling my career progression, having innovative ideas ignored, and experiencing escalated microaggressions.

So yeah. She tried it.

Both managers and employees understand the need to conceal our authentic selves, and statistics illustrate the dangers of asking for authenticity. A 2022 study published in the Journal of Applied Psychology found that people of color are more likely to hide their authentic selves to appear less different from white coworkers.[8] For Black people in the workplace, this often looks like code switching, wearing straight hair or a wig, and keeping silent about covert and overt racism in the workplace.

Here are a few reasons why we do it:

<u>Fear of judgment</u>. Judgements from colleagues can be intimidating and may jeopardize relationships necessary to get work done smoothly.

---

[8] Umoh, Ruth. 2024. "Newly Hired Black Workers Face Greater Scrutiny From Their Bosses, Study Finds." Fortune, January 31, 2024. https://fortune.com/2024/01/31/black-workers-new-hires-scrutiny-fired-unemployment/.

[8] Hewlett, Sylvia Ann. 2014. "Too Many People of Color Feel Uncomfortable at Work." Harvard Business Review. August 7, 2014. https://hbr.org/2012/10/too-many-people-of-color-feel#:~:text=Overall%2C%20people%20of%20color%20are,African%2DAmerican%20network%20TV%20manager.

Lack of psychological safety. The inherent lack of trust and safe space to make mistakes compounds insecurities about freely discussing mental health struggles, disclosing disabilities requiring accommodations, or suggesting divergent ideas without ridicule.[8]

Wanting to "fit in." Within the workplace, these often show up as hiding quirky passions, nerdy personality traits, introversion, or extroversion tendencies that could perceive us as misfits among our colleagues.

Imposter syndrome. An alarming number of professionals grapple with perpetual self-doubt in their capabilities or adequate performance to justify their roles. This ferments imposter syndrome, causing intense psychological strain and a lack of trust in one's competence.

Risk of adverse impact. People conceal aspects of themselves to allay fears of losing out on leadership opportunities or even facing termination if these traits become public knowledge.

While this has been deemed a self-preservation strategy to navigate corporate America, it's taking a toll on our mental and physical health.

According to a recent Yale School of Medicine article, Black women experience sustained physiological challenges from navigating multiple forms of racism and sexism, which cause physiological deterioration or

---

[8] Henneborn, Laurie. 2021. "Make It Safe for Employees to Disclose Their Disabilities." Harvard Business Review. September 13, 2021. https://hbr.org/2021/06/make-it-safe-for-employees-to-disclose-their-disabilities.

'weathering' of the body at young ages."[8] Researchers found that by age 50, Black women show substantially higher levels of inflammation and regulation of over 100 genes associated with illnesses, comparable to white women who are 20 years older. This disproportionate physical stress contributes to high rates of chronic disease early in life.

Another study found evidence that Black men who experienced longer durations of economic hardship and discrimination based on their race had a higher risk of early-onset chronic illness and aging-related cell changes compared to Black men without similar exposures.[8]

The cumulative toll of hiding our authentic selves to survive toxic work climates is real and destructive. As the research shows, the sustained stress of inauthenticity is taking a toll on our mental health, speeding our aging process, and causing disease. Though adaptations like code-switching or straightening hair might seem harmless, the underlying reason—to mitigate racism, sexism, and other prejudices—means these masking behaviors still exact a heavy price on our health and well-being.

---

[8] Yup, Kayla. 2022. "Black Women Excluded From Critical Studies Due to 'Weathering.'" Yale School of Medicine. December 1, 2022. https://medicine.yale.edu/news-article/black-women-excluded-from-critical-studies-due-to-weathering/.

[8] Allen, Julie Ober, Daphne C. Watkins, Linda M. Chatters, Arline T. Geronimus, and Vicki Johnson-Lawrence. 2019. "Cortisol and Racial Health Disparities Affecting Black Men in Later Life: Evidence From MIDUS II." American Journal of Men's Health 13 (4): 155798831987096. https://doi.org/10.1177/1557988319870969.

How Authenticity Looks

Embrace the strength within your roots, for in the tapestry of self-identity, each thread weaves a powerful narrative of resilience and pride.
—Coach Barnes

Developing a strong sense of self-identity and expanding self-awareness are key to minimizing the harmful effects of denying our authentic selves. Self-identity determines our driving motivations and what we stand for at the core—summed up in what thought leaders often call your "why statement." It provides deeper wisdom around our needs, emotions, strengths, and desires to set healthy boundaries.

Fortifying self-awareness as a complement requires turning inward to recognize triggers, insecurities, communication styles, and emotional patterns. What specific situations reliably cue stress responses like fight-flight-freeze-fawn due to past wounds or trauma? How do compulsive over-apologizing or people-pleasing instincts signal lingering self-worth issues? By patiently exploring this through journaling or counseling, you gain the power to respond consciously rather than react unconsciously.

By working on both, you develop:

<u>A clear self-identity</u>. This leads to communication that is grounded in your core values, priorities, and sense of purpose, regardless of what's going on around you. When you have a solid inner foundation, you rely less on external cues about how to show up. This makes it easier to retain your authentic communication styles, hairstyles, etc., even when they go against workplace cultural norms.

Expanded self-awareness. Becoming more self-aware builds an understanding of what situations tap into your insecurities. You gain insight into moments and conversations when you feel most vulnerable to others' judgments or scrutiny. You can then anticipate these stressful situations and intentionally center yourself on self-compassion as a buffer.

Deeper knowledge of your emotional patterns. Strengthening your emotional intelligence helps you recognize early on when you have slipped into people-pleasing, masking, or hiding behaviors in hopes of securing approval or allaying judgment. This allows you to catch yourself over-adapting and course-correcting yourself so that you are in alignment with your identity and needs.

Authenticity, even in restrictive environments. As Brené Brown warns, the most dangerous ideologies package oppression as wisdom. Wisdom, however, comes from within and doesn't require external validation. Anchoring ourselves in our inner light enables us to clearly evaluate situations and, as a result, move authentically.

I was working in an environment that sucked the warmth out of the building and the life out of my spirit. I felt defeated, tired, and lifeless. Karen — the comfort and authenticity police — was stealing the joy of coming to work and doing what I loved—working with children and families and shaping the minds of future leaders. Don't let anyone steal your joy.

For years, Karen and I were at odds on several issues. But it was this situation that motivated me to seek a better way of handling things.

There were continuous meetings when my ideas were later stolen in front of my eyes —"Christina" Columbused"— as if I could not distinguish my suggestions from a white-washed paraphrase. I no longer found solace in being there. But I knew I had to determine what showing up and remaining true to myself meant. To do that, I had to determine what was more important to me: proving Karen wrong or doing my job.

Should I continue to focus my efforts on correcting my manager's problematic behaviors? Doing so only led to disagreements and tension. I wasn't getting anywhere. My other option was to focus on finding fulfillment in simply doing my job. I was in a career that I loved, and I couldn't imagine doing anything else. And I couldn't deny the impact we made on the students; I enjoyed talking with the parents; and I loved working in a predominantly Black school. I eventually realized that changing others was outside my control. Instead, I reclaimed my power by doing what she asked me to do — showing up authentically. By focusing inward, I developed a strong sense of self-identity and expanded my self-awareness. And when I did, I got my joy back.

The first thing I did was change how I communicated with Karen. Rather than offering my ideas freely only to have them disregarded and regurgitated, I shifted my approach. When Karen asked for suggestions, my new response was, "Why don't you share your ideas first, and we can build from there?" By stepping back as the idea generator, I regained authority over how I engaged.

Focusing my energy on fulfilling my professional responsibilities rather than seeking validation or attempting to change others' problematic behaviors was an empowering step towards authenticity. This act of focusing on my purpose as an educator working with children—my "why"— strengthened my self-identity. Rather than allowing external factors to steer my sense of purpose and joy, I reconnected with my internal motivations.

Focusing inward also enhanced my self-awareness. I gained clarity about boundaries and where I did and didn't have agency. I recognized that exerting efforts to change or convince my manager was an exercise in futility that drained my energy. This self-insight about my sphere of influence and control oriented my attention toward what I could impact. It also helped illuminate my emotional triggers. My experiences with having my ideas rejected or stolen touched on deeper wounds of invalidation and erasure. This made me more aware of my self-worth and helped me recognize that my voice was worth hearing. I started to advocate for myself and find ways to communicate without feeling powerless. I also became more aware of my interactions with others and the energy I brought to conversations. This paved the way for me to maintain my authentic self and find fulfillment even in an unsupportive environment. The journey of self-discovery gave me tools to define myself rather than be defined by others' limited perspectives.

Taking ownership of your self-identity and developing self-awareness are ongoing journeys that require dedication and courage. If you're facing a similar crossroads, ask yourself these reflective questions to bolster your sense of purpose and strengthen your knowledge of emotional patterns.

Self-Identity

1. What are your core values?
2. What is your purpose in life?
3. What is your plan for the future?
4. What principles do you stand by, no matter what?

Self-Awareness

1. Do you react to disappointment by addressing issues directly or deflecting pain?
2. Given what you know about stress now, what would you tell your younger self?
3. What boundaries or self-care habits could you implement to build resilience?
4. In what area do you need to grow emotionally the most?
5. How do you feel when faced with change?
6. Do you believe in giving second chances?
7. What is your greatest strength, and why?
8. How often do you ask others for help?

THE CALL FOR AUTHENTICITY

"You've got to learn to leave the table when love's no longer being served."
—Nina Simone

Karen and I continued to work together until she moved on to a new position. She was replaced by a dashiki-wearing Black woman.

Ironically, she was mentally shackled to an oppressive mindset and operated just like Karen. And she ended up dismantling the last essence of Black community teachers and staff we had left. By that time, my illness had taken over, and I was no longer willing to allow the darkness of stress to penetrate my peace and mental well-being. For me, protecting my peace in the workplace meant knowing when to walk away.

As you embark on your workplace journey as a team member or leader, I offer the following advice: lead with love. When I started my coaching business, I was determined not to be the kind of leader I had encountered over the years. Thus, I grounded myself in the following principles: truth, peace, transparency, and balance. You can do the same wherever you work, in any job you perform.

Determine what each of the principles above means to you, or define your own. When you do, your vision of an authentic, peaceful leader will become clear. Then strive to live by those principles. Through them, you can create a culture that is based on trust and respect, where everyone is valued and can thrive. Remember:

People feel comfortable being themselves in a peaceful work environment based on trust and respect. People can share ideas openly without fear of judgment or retaliation when there is less conflict, drama, or politics. This supports authentic self-expression.

People tend to perceive leaders who cultivate a calm and understanding work culture as more genuine and sincere. If leaders have open communication, admit mistakes, listen to feedback, and prioritize employee well-being, people are more likely to view them as authentic. Again, as a leader, you will need to determine what this looks and feels like for the workplace culture you are aiming to build.

Companies that value work-life balance, diversity, and inclusion help employees integrate their personal and professional identities. Policies that support employees' physical and emotional needs allow people to show up more fully as themselves without feeling the need to compartmentalize different aspects of self.

Workplaces characterized by psychological safety, where people aren't afraid to take interpersonal risks, create environments where employees can share their true perspectives easier. Feeling assured that your vulnerabilities won't be held against you promotes authentic conversations.

Non-hierarchical workplaces with collaborative norms can foster authenticity by valuing all voices equally. When decisions are made democratically and ideas can come from anyone, people are empowered to contribute in their authentic way.

The journey to embracing authenticity in the workplace is complex and ongoing. Yet, we can cultivate genuine self-expression by growing our self-knowledge and centering our inner light to navigate repressive spaces. As leaders, we shape the path ahead through the cultures we create and the norms we challenge. And being authentic means that staff can stand fully for who they are. My hope is that we each find fulfillment and purpose while bringing our complete selves to uplift our teams and organizations. The world needs the full measure of our collective brilliance.

Xenia Barnes leverages behavioral analysis and community activism experience as a dynamic speaker, author, and trauma coach to transform domestic abuse, gun violence, and illness survivors. A PhD candidate, her acclaimed talk on psychology safety promotes and inspires audiences to love themselves through trauma. Her coaching polishes inner gems so teams can enhance performance via strategic thinking, smart management, efficient planning, and essential training.

Visit xeniabarnes.com.

REFLECTION QUESTIONS

1. How can you stay true to your authentic self while navigating the challenges and expectations of the workplace?

REFLECTION QUESTIONS

2. In what ways can self-awareness and emotional intelligence help you navigate difficult professional relationships?

REFLECTION QUESTIONS

3. How can you create a work environment that fosters authenticity, psychological safety, and inclusivity for all employees?

Let's Stay in Touch

Looking for more self-help reads?

The Author's Journey is an award-winning author marketing agency with a hybrid publishing arm. We publish nonfiction books and anthologies penned by industry thought leaders covering a wide range of topics.

Visit us at:

https://theauthorsjourney.co/books

www.linkedin.com/in/elonawashington

www.ingramcontent.com/pod-product-compliance
Lightning Source LLC
Chambersburg PA
CBHW051620010526
44119CB00009B/218